SOMEBODY I USED TO LOVE

NAVNEET NISHANT

An imprint of
Srishti Publishers & Distributors

Srishti Publishers & Distributors

A unit of AJR Publishing LLP

212A, Peacock Lane

Shahpur Jat, New Delhi – 110 049

editorial@srishtipublishers.com

First Published in India by Launchpad,
an imprint of Srishti Publishers & Distributors in 2025

Printed and Bound in India.

*"When I was walking down the way,
with shattered dreams in my head,
I started living a dream, a dream that I never had,
I walked through the days, I walked through the years
Until the dream that was broken once melted into tears."*
@TheArtHippo

PREFACE

'Who are you, Nav?' her gentle voice snapped me out of my wandering thoughts.

'I am Nav…,' I paused. 'An artist. A dad. A partner. A friend, among many other things,' I replied.

I found that question to be rhetorical. It was not my first time sitting across the glass table from my therapist in that minimalist and professional-looking clinic. It wasn't the first time we were meeting each other.

I had always imagined therapy as an intimate, cosy conversation in a detached space from the outside world. This place, Daffodil Studios, gave the same feeling. Over the period I had been seeing my therapist, she had become a fan of my work. One side of her clinic (studio) wall was just my works, with a vine growing through it on a hanging planter. I liked that place. It called itself a studio, not a clinic.

'It's been two years we have been seeing each other now,' she said, and I nodded, watching outside the window. Kids were playing.

'And you know you come here only because you like coming here? There is not much you have done over the last two years that can be considered progress, right?' she added.

'Well, I like you,' I said, trying to flirt with her. 'And I like the view from your window.'

'Something is different about you today,' she said. 'How have you been feeling since our last session?'

'Great, actually! Glad you asked,' I snapped back to the room and said what I had been waiting to speak to her for some time.

'I finished it, doc,' I said with a broad smile, and she asked the obvious question.

'Finished what?'

'The book that I wrote 16 years ago.'

She fell silent. After a pause, she asked if I would be comfortable sharing the ending.

'I think I would like to share it with everyone, I guess,' I told her.

'What did you call the ending?' she asked.

'A new chapter,' I replied.

***

What you'll read hereafter are words written over a decade ago, 16 years to be precise. It was never published because I didn't know how the story ended.

Sixteen years later, in hindsight, it makes sense.

The 30,000 words or so you will read have been a part of my suppressed memory for over a decade—a long decade of battling with addiction, depression and anxiety.

Now with grey hair, a beautiful daughter, and a life battling harsh winters in Canada, as I add the last chapter, I realize I have aged. But the real author of this book was a teenager, a naïve, a romantic and a fool.

I hope you find joy in his writing and his world.

PART I

(DIAMONDS)

Chapter 1
The Beginning

Summer 2005

It was the most charming place I had ever laid eyes on at the age of 18. Having grown up in a village, I was a product of an all-boys boarding school in a less educated and underdeveloped part of India. During childhood, my town was infamous for its corrupt politicians, bandits hiding in its lush green forests, and a large population struggling with the scarcity of electricity.

I come from an era when kids still played in the street. It is tough to believe, but just over three decades ago, gaming meant Mario and Contra. What was better than an audio cassette was a VCR. MTV was music for the world, and Tom and Jerry were every kid's dream. Driving cars without seat belts and motorbikes without helmets was okay—a world before fitness watches, iPhones, Instagram and TikTok. Public Internet was still making its way into India through cybercafes.

The setting for this story is Jamshedpur, reachable by an overnight train ride from my village. It's a city established by one of India's wealthiest industrialist families—the same family that owns Land Rover and Jaguar. The city's cool nickname was "Tata."

Before reaching this point in life, I had spent my formative years shuttling between different boarding schools, as my Dad was determined to provide both his children with an education for a brighter future. In post-independence India, as the middle class sought stability, the top career choices imposed on kids of my generation were becoming a doctor, lawyer, engineer, or a government job. I chose engineering and kind of followed suit with my brother.

My brother, six years older than me and armed with his engineering degree, was my guiding force. In the summer of 2005, before navigation systems, on that particular day when this story started, he served as my personal GPS in Tata. The city amazed me with its clean streets, wide roads, and houses that seemed to adhere to blueprints. For someone more familiar with hostel rooms and rural landscapes than the three colours of traffic signals, it felt like stepping onto a movie set. There was no mud, no chaotic construction—just orderly, numbered streets and people waiting for buses at bus stops. It was a revolution in my perception of urban life.

Our mission that day was to locate the Brar residence in the heart of a Punjabi colony. Imagine turbans in every colour imaginable, dupattas fluttering like flags, and kids joyfully chasing each other through the streets while their parents engaged in lively conversations. Stepping onto that street felt like entering a vibrant painting bursting with life.

We finally located the right house. After pushing the round white button and a ding-dong later, a thin, frail man's silhouette questioned our presence inside the window next to the door. My brother explained that we were referred there by the coaching centre. I enrolled in a coaching centre in Tata to prepare for the big engineering exams. That was my primary purpose in seeking a year-long accommodation as a paying guest. I heard a mumble, the door opened, and an old man, a character straight out of a kids' cartoon, with his tight turban that tugged his eyes up by the edges, welcomed us in. He could have been a museum exhibit on wrinkles.

He offered us refreshments. As we were building up with small talk, my brother called him "Sardar ji," which seemed to raise the man's eyebrow higher than I thought physically possible. *Mental note: Avoid 'Sardar ji'.*

As we learned, this delightful old man wasn't typically the point person for such matters – that was his son's responsibility. However, with the son and daughter-in-law away, he had assumed the temporary role of captain of the ship.

I requested to see my room on the ground floor with a separate entrance and a window providing a front-row seat to the pretty neighbourhood. As I opened the door, the air was thick with the scent of paint and old wood, oddly comforting. The view included another old man with a handcart of clothes to be ironed under a banyan tree. He had such kind eyes that you usually don't see every day. The smile he carried could light that dimly lit room. The room, although dusty, was spacious, appearing to have been in hibernation for months.

After ensuring my comfort, my brother departed, satisfied with the arrangement. He had his own life. The host, also acting as a chef for the day, insisted on cooking lunch, revealing that starting the next day, I would be enjoying the culinary skills of his daughter-in-law. Apparently, living there came with a mandatory 'tiffin service'. It was a comprehensive paying guest arrangement with a nearby market and bus stop. What a perfect location!

Diary Entry: 06 June 2005

I moved to Jamshedpur today. It's a bit different from my hostel, but then again, I guess change is bound to happen in life. I feel lonely here; I suppose I will settle and find some friends as soon as the classes at the coaching institute start. This place is big and good, and the food is simply fantastic. The colony is charming, but I hardly see anyone my age here. I love the window in my room; I can sit and watch the kids play in the street. Today, while I watched them play, it reminded me of my childhood.

Tomorrow, I will go to the coaching institute and get some reading material; maybe if I start studying something, I'll keep myself busy.

All good energies in this new chapter of my life.

Chapter 2
The Blooming

So, there I was, every evening, stationed at my usual spot by the window, presiding as the unofficial judge of the neighbourhood's Olympic-level hopscotch championship. However, on this particular evening, there was a palpable shift in the atmosphere. The sky adorned itself in a new violet and orange ensemble, and a mischievous breeze seemed determined to tousle my hair. It was like the universe was orchestrating a spectacle, and I had a front-row seat.

It had been a few weeks since I moved to this place, and I had liked my new setup so far. The landlady was friendly. She cooked good food. Her whole family was charming. There was a particular rhythm to life in that colony. The old man would get up every morning at five and go to get milk. He would be joined in by fellow morning walkers. The bustle of kids going to school and grownups rushing to work would start the day. As that wave settled, housewives would charm the colony, buying vegetables and bread from the street vendors that would come every day, talking loudly and holding all sorts of conversations from their respective houses while drying out clothes in the sun. The afternoon would be a lull, but then the kids would get back from school, adults from wherever they went, and every evening would be a celebration with children playing in the street and families laughing loudly.

That evening, lost in my own world, gazing out blissfully, I was unaware of the outside world. That's when it happened. Out of nowhere, a head popped up from under my window like a jack-in-the-box! Maximum surprise level achieved. I'm pretty sure I invented a new dance move as I recoiled in my chair. There she stood—a curly-haired intruder in my personal space, wearing a perfume that declared, 'I'm here to haunt your senses.'

We locked eyes—hers big and curious, mine wide with a 'what on earth' expression. Her face was something out of a fairy tale, and I was thinking, "Is this a princess or a ninja? How did she sneak in without me noticing?" Her thin, little glossy lips had a dot on them, and she was keeping them shut tight. Her face was fresh like a morning rose. Everything about her and that moment was unbelievably perfect.

Then came the moment of truth. "Got you," someone said. She was a hide-and-seek fugitive—caught! I must've missed the memo on the neighbourhood's covert operations. She must have jumped over the fence right in front of me.

As our locked gaze ended with her being discovered, I was unsure if it was because she expected a response in that momentary window or she found something odd; she said, "How weird!" and returned to the playing gang. Ouch. Right in the male ego. What did I do? Just because I got lost in her eyes? I slammed the window so hard it almost gave the glass a crisis. But, you know, curiosity killed the cat and wounded the ego, so I peeked again. Poof! She vanished like a ninja after a smoke bomb trick.

I had not seen her before. Her words echoed in my head, her perfume lingering like a stubborn houseguest. If she had wings, I'd have sworn she was an undercover angel on a field trip.

I turned detective and raced to the roof for a better view. And there she was, arguing with kids half her size in a scarlet suit, like a pint-sized fashionista among minions. She was waving her hair and mauve dupatta like flags of rebellion in a kiddie coup, arguing about something.

I made sure she didn't catch me gawking. My bruised ego was in recovery, after all. But then, the plot twist – she stomps off

from the game, throwing a tantrum that could win awards, declaring a lifetime ban on playing with those 'cheating' kids. As she stormed off, she glanced back at my window.

Diary Entry: 14 June 2005

Today, I saw a girl, an angel without wings—beautiful and naive. She was playing in the street with the kids. She felt like butterflies and bunnies—you know the feeling you get when they are around. The way she was fighting with the kids, the way she was angry with them, and the way she left the game—it was all so dramatic.

I hope to see her again tomorrow. The way she fought with the kids, I'm sure she lives somewhere nearby.

I feel good that she looked back once before leaving the game. She noticed. I need a good haircut.

Chapter 3
Curious Case of
the Mystery Girl

I found myself grilling the sole person in the colony with the all-access pass – my landlady's six-year-old daughter, Kamal. You'd be surprised how much intelligence a six-year-old can possess. Picture this: a grown adult extracting top-secret intel from a kid who likely still believes in the Tooth Fairy. But desperate times call for desperate measures.

"Why's your mom so hung up about that girl?" I ventured, attempting to sound casual. Let's be honest, though – I was as casual as a cat on a hot tin roof. She could have swung either way. Following my last rendezvous with the mystery girl, I had a conversation with my landlady, who casually slipped in this condition while explaining house rules: 'Thou shall not engage with that girl three doors down across the street in any way; she is bad news, Kapish.'

Kamal, the pint-sized human with the attention span of a goldfish, was more intrigued by my digital watch. "Mummy says she's bad news," she said, eyes fixed on the blinking lights of the watch. She was the second person to mention that to me.

"And why's that?" I prodded, handing her my watch as a bribe.

"Because the guy who stayed with us before you fell for her," she blurted out, eyes now as wide as saucers. Dramatically, she whispered, "Her dad caught him, and, let's just say, it wasn't pretty. Our families had a brawl about it."

"Her dad beat the guy? Like a fight and all? Violent?" I asked.

"He's a weightlifter," she declared as if that explained everything. Great, just my luck. There's a girl I'm not supposed to look at, and she has a dad who can probably bench-press a car, and my paying guest rules handbook boldly outlines 'no-interaction' as a condition.

"The guy who lived here before you, we had to ask him to leave within two days after all that happened. We have become a neighbourhood gossip item. Mom really wants to avoid it," Kamal continued.

"Who else is in her family?" I continued my not-so-subtle interrogation.

"Her mom, grandpa, dad, and sister," she replied, randomly listing them like items on a grocery list.

"Her name is Nitika, right?"

"Nitika? No, it's Ami. Ahmanpreet Gill," she corrected me. And there, I finally had the name. "But it is pronounced a little differently. More like Ahmi," she continued.

Think of the two most common sounds you make when you're indecisive: 'Ah' when you're pondering your options and 'Mmm' when you're thinking about something delicious. Now, just add a cheerful 'ee' as if you've just had a lightbulb moment. Put them together, and you have 'Ah-mmm-ee' — that's how Komal would pronounce it. It was like going from hesitation to contemplation to elation, all in one short name. Ami.

"Ah, ok," I shrugged, pretending like I didn't care. I changed the subject to the intricate workings of my digital watch, and she seemed to forget the whole conversation. I like the goldfish in kids.

Diary Entry: Sneaky Peeks and Award weeks

So, there's this girl. Her name is Ami. And she's got this habit of moonwalking down my street – yeah, not just in my daydreams. And get this: she's always sneaking, and whenever she crosses my window, she looks directly into my window. Spy much? It's been a couple of weeks since she started her little espionage mission. A couple of weeks since I first saw her. At first, I thought, "Oh, she's just curious," but her face? it screamed, "I'm up to something!"

Days turned into a staring contest. Evenings fell into a routine where she played outside until darkness enveloped everything, and I would remain ensconced in my room, watching her from my window with the lights off. The strategy was to shield myself from the potential scrutiny of the tyrants on both sides of the road that divided our houses. However, one night, as she embarked on her customary walk-by, I decided to break the pattern and switched

the lights ON. Surprise! It was like catching a ninja in the act. She shot me this "how dare you?" look, followed by a series of facial expressions I still can't decipher, and then – poof – she vanished.

Most evenings that summer, I assumed the role of Captain Awkward, stationed by my window, eagerly anticipating the sequel. My life morphed into a string of evenings devoted to the game of 'Spot the Mystery Girl'. I'd attempt a smile, only to back out at the last moment. I'd interpret her expressions like a perplexed detective. And believe it or not, I began making bets with myself: "Finish this assignment, and perhaps she'll make an appearance." Yeah, it was totally normal.

Every weekday, there she was, in her school uniform, exuding innocence, stealing glances inconspicuously. For a fleeting moment, our eyes would meet – her with a knockoff Nike bag and a water bottle sitting in that autorickshaw. She was every bit of the girl of my dreams. She was elegant and graceful and always carried a pixie-like twinkle in her eyes.

Our silent movie transitioned from mere glances to shy smiles as time progressed. Talking? Nah, we were both too chicken for that.

You know what they say, "Love's loudest words are spoken with silent stares." Or something like that. It took us the entire summer to progress from glances to smiles.

Chapter 4
Trouble In Teen Town

Autumn And Winter 2005

So, there I was, living the laid-back life in my not-so-new accommodation, a kind of familiar neighbourhood, and at the cusp of another glimpse of her when my landlady barges in, grinning like she's hit the jackpot. Turns out, she had landed a new cash cow, uh, tenant. "Great," I thought, "competition for Ami's attention. Just what I needed."

Enter Pankaj – PK, a guy so dark and eccentric that I wondered if he was part human, part shadow—always grinning like the Joker's long-lost cousin. It was as if his face had forgotten how to make other expressions. Despite being as introverted as a hermit crab, both of us clicked. Thanks to PK, I now had roof access for my top-secret 'Operation: Watch Ami'. His room was the only thing on one edge of the house's first floor, while I lived on the ground floor.

PK, bless his nerd soul, wasn't into Ami. He was too busy worshipping at the altar of IITs, NITs, and other engineering institutes I couldn't even pronounce. He was a super-nerd, a super nice guy, the kind you don't mind having around.

Things got interesting. PK and I would hang out on the roof, doing nothing, while Ami pranced around in her garden, smiling sneakily at me. She had this ninja move: walking behind her mom to hide her smile. Those evenings were like fast-forwarding through a movie: crisp, fresh autumn evenings, days getting cooler, trees casting longer shadows.

I was the king of the roof, watching Ami water her plants like they were in a desert. Seriously, those plants were drowning in attention. Sometimes, she would hold placards in her hand and walk in a circle on her little front porch, pretending to study but passing me smiles.

Soon, winter came, and so did another cash cow for the lucky landlady, but this time, my nemesis, Sam – Mr Tall, Dark, and Handsome. Running out of space, my landlady shoved PK into my room and gave Sam the penthouse suite. Great, that was just what I needed: a Greek God for a neighbour with the rooftop access pass I had just lost.

Sam was a worthy opponent. He had his eyes on Ami from day one. Within two days of settling in and getting friendly to PK and me, he had asked about the girl with the curly hair. Within a week, he was fully aware of when and how to spot Ami. He'd do this ridiculous morning ritual those winter mornings, standing in the sun, pretending to study, while actually just watching Ami leave in her autorickshaw. Little did he know, Ami was just fond of me. I mean, I didn't know for sure as we had never talked till then, but at the same time, when Sam would watch her from the roof, I would lock eyes with this girl for a fleeting moment from my window downstairs, and her eyes said 'I see you'.

I quickly realized there was some weird love geometry—me, Ami, and Sam. It was not a triangle yet, but there was definitely some geometry there.

Our little teen drama got an upgrade with the introduction of Sam. He was the new roof preacher in the colony. Ami's mom, that well-built lady, wife to the boxer and weightlifter, turned into a full-time neighbourhood watch commander. She obviously grew aware of the heightened activity from the rival house. The winter unfolded like Big Brother but with nosier moms and less privacy.

Ami's mom was so into her new hobby of guarding the gates that I swear she could give the Secret Service a run for their money. She would come to the door and scan outside every time Ami left the door. If Ami were out, she would be there waiting five minutes before Ami's arrival. If Ami would play in the evening, her mom would pull a chair and sit on the front porch to keep an eye on her. And Sam? The dude thought he was in a movie, posing on the roof every morning like he was auditioning for the role of a brooding hero in a low-budget romance flick. This, of course, made my life a living sitcom episode.

My now-roommate PK decided to play detective one day and hit me with the big question, "Do you like her?" As if I was going to spill my secrets while standing in my not-so-glamorous spot. I tried to play it cool, but inside, I was like a mixtape on repeat, all about Ami.

Then there was this winter evening; she was walking in front of my window in jeans and a crop top and constantly looking at me every time she crossed, but to no end. Fortunately, her mom was not around, so the little girl gathered all her courage and attempted to communicate via hand gestures.

Pass 1: Her hand moved like an aeroplane – whoosh! From below her waistline upwards to her tummy.

Pass 2: She made a house-looking triangle with both her hands.

Pass 3: She gave me a frustrated look, saying, 'Why you no understand human!'

Pass 4: She runs like Flash and does a quick sketch of running by moving her hands fast.

Pass 10: Sad smiley on my face saying, 'I am trying hard to understand what you are saying, but I have no idea what it means.'

This routine of her trials and my failures at understanding continued for about ten attempts or so until she sensed her mom coming out. I was dumb enough not to comprehend what she tried so hard to explain. Poor me. Poor her. She went back inside.

Sam was perched on the roof, as always, and I am sure he saw she was trying to interact with me. It must have broken his heart, and at least I had that as a win!

For the next week, I kept staring outside through my window of opportunity (literally), but she was nowhere to be seen. I kept on thinking what she might have been trying to say. Was she asking me to go away from here because her father might have come to know something about me, and that's what was holding her inside the house? Or maybe she was telling me she was going away for some time.

I turned into a part-time window-gazer full-time daydreamer for the entire week, waiting for Ami's next performance. PK then decides to state the obvious, "Dude, you're so in love." Thanks, Captain Obvious! I tried to deny it, but it was like hiding an elephant in a mini-fridge.

Then PK drops another bomb – Sam thinks Ami likes him. Cue dramatic music and my world crashes down! In my panic, I accidentally confessed, "She smiles at me, not him!" Oops, my secret's out, and PK's got this 'I knew it' grin on his face.

I was caught in my own web of denials, blushing like a tomato. And PK? He just smiled, probably thinking, 'This gets better now.'

Chapter 5
Vacations and
The Breakthrough

2006

Two weeks had passed, and so had my vacation. While I was back with my folks, the only thing on my mind all the time was Ami. I hadn't seen Ami the week before returning to my hometown. I spent those days in a dilemma, wondering if she had gone somewhere or if her dad was now aware of our relationship, signalling the need to hide. On the day the train arrived at Tata station just before dawn, I had one thing on my mind: 'Will she be there when I get to my Paying Guest accommodation?' The air had a lovely winter nip as I walked towards my house with a bag on my back, but my eyes were fixed on the windows of her house.

Knock, knock! Once, twice, thrice. Just as I was about to bang on the door, I heard a drunken, muffled voice.

'Who is this?'

'It's me, PK!' I yelled out.

My room! It was a mess. PK himself was a mess. I knew he couldn't live in a clean place, and I should have guessed that if he lived somewhere, that place couldn't have been clean for more than a week.

'What have you been doing here?'

'What have you got to do with it? I do many things when I am alone.' He continued with an unfriendly yawn while slipping back inside his blanket. It was 5 am in the morning. 'So, how was the trip, and how's everyone in the village?'

'Fine. You know how I enjoy my home.' I said.

'Ya ya! I know you're a grown-up homesick baby!'

'Ah,' I wanted to punch him in his sleep and ask him a million questions. I resisted the punch and said, 'Okay, tell me, is she back yet? Did you see her?'

'Yes, she is back and has already badly broken a heart here. But can't we talk about all this when I wake up again?' He was mumbling in sleep, but from whatever I had just gathered, this sure was interesting.

'No, we can't!' I jumped in excitement, pushed my bag aside, opened my shoes, removed a hell of a lot of things from my untidy bed, and slipped inside my blanket, all in a fraction of a second, waiting for him to elaborate on his statement.

'But I can't talk right now. You are the love-struck, homesick baby traveller; for me, this is midnight. You can wait by my bed, begging on your knees till I wake up.'

He was serious. Within five minutes, he was snoring, and I was wide awake. I knew I would have to wait until morning, and so I did. There was no other way around it; he was like that. When in demand, he was stubborn. Son of a bitch!

I kept imagining what it could be and then fell into a deep slumber.

'Wake up, my homie boy! Lunchtime.'

I opened my eyes, now red and aching. PK was towering over me. Sam was also around but just said 'hi' with a quite formal expression. Though he was never a great friend of mine, his constipated look was still unfamiliar. Strange!

I looked at PK, but the way he was behaving 'over' normal made me judge that it was not the right time for me to ask whatever the hell he had left unexplained in the morning. Quite a pig he was.

"Where is my cell phone?" I asked Sam. I had left it with him before going home, as he had asked for it.

"Oh yes! Here, if you get any calls for me, please let me know," he said, pulling out my Motorola C350 handset from his jacket pocket.

"Why are you putting your pearls on display?" I saw PK grinning.

"Nothing," PK replied quickly, hiding his grin.

We had our lunch in the quietest manner I could imagine. Sam was silent like a funeral drum, and PK passed a dumb smile to himself every now and then, making small talk about how good the landlady cooked.

After lunch, Sam took PK in a corner and murmured something in deep secrecy; he left for his room immediately after that. There was no usual chit-chat; he didn't even ask me how my trip was! Five seconds passed, and PK bounced to bolt our door from inside.

"You know what happened?"

"Speak up, bastard!"

"Okay, then listen to this, bastard! Sam asked her out while you were gone."

"What! How? I mean, how did he reach her? When? What happened? Tell me the whole story." While I couldn't talk to her even once, even when I knew there was something in her heart for me, he had already asked her out! That was unbelievable for me.

"Easy dude, easy..." PK went on at his own pace. "One evening, both of us were standing on the roof. He had your cell phone that he had borrowed when you were gone. She was back from wherever she had gone the week before and was probably waiting to see you."

"How do you know she was waiting for me?" I wanted to know the whole story in one line.

"Shut up, loser! Don't interrupt when I am talking. You always want to hear that she likes you, isn't it? Anyway, here is what happened. He was eyeing her, and she was looking for you. He thought she was looking at him, and so we had a bet. Fortunately, all her family's boxers, weight lifters, and WWF fighters were inside the house, and she was the only one out. The street was silent, too. I guess the New Year's downtime gave us peace. The bet was to go to her main gate and give her the cell number to contact him."

"Wow! Then?"

"With extraterrestrial confidence, Sam went with the number written on a piece of paper and gave it to her. She didn't seem shocked, as I would have imagined her to be. Instead, she told him she could not call him; she didn't have access to a phone. She asked him to meet her at the city stadium the next evening at 5."

"What?" and a blade went straight through my heart. How could she call him to meet her when she liked me? Maybe all this was just a drama. Moments like these are amazing; thousands of possibilities and stories crossed my mind in that fraction of a second he took between his last and the next sentence. My heart was pounding.

"Okay, okay! You need to know the end, but I will go by the line only. He met her the next evening in all the best dresses, perfumes, and hairstyles he could. He wore your shirt also. Anyway, dude, could you have imagined that she is a national athlete?"

"Nope," I said in a depressed tone; I was more interested in knowing the end.

"And she is a class XI student."

"What?" This made me jump out of bed! This was too much for me to take in a single day! If she was in high school, why the hell had my landlady told me that she was in school?

"Ya dude, this is the fact. I think the landlady said all this just to keep us away from her. These two families have a big dispute because of the guy who lived here before we moved in." I remembered Kamal telling me something of this sort about the guy who lived at that place before us, how Ami's father and all thrashed him up.

"Okay, whatever, tell me the whole thing," he had my complete attention again.

"Yes! So Sam went there, quite happy, and sat for almost one hour just watching her on the tracks. Though Sam was a bit disappointed by the selection of this strange place for his first date, he was very happy at the thought of having finally won both the battles: the cold war with you and the girl. PK's eyes sparkled evil, and he banged his right fist into his left palm, saying, 'But bang! He was wrong. She had called him there only because she wanted to know more about you. After all, she wanted to contact you."

My eyes were wide; my heart beat faster, and as they say, I guess I skipped a few beats. In my whole life, nothing like this had ever happened.

"Yes, dude, I know there are a lot of surprises for you today, but before Sam could actually talk anything cheesy or ask her out, she told him frankly that they can only be friends, and she wanted to contact you through him. That bastard, he was furious, and he left."

"What a bastard!" I agreed with whatever PK said that day and with the same intensity of excitement with which he was telling. I was excited!

"He has asked me not to tell you anything; that's what he reminded me of in the corner after lunch."

Puff! "I am happy, PK. Do you think I should go ahead with this?"

"Of course, you should, dude, don't underestimate yourself. You are good, too good. You deserve a good girl like her."

"I am scared."

"You are scared without reason; do what you want. And yes, don't tell Sam anything about what I have told you. He still thinks she might call on your number for him someday." That made me understand what Sam meant about telling him if anyone called for him when he gave me the phone back.

I looked at PK, and he looked at me. A secrecy-loaded shared smile filled the whole room.

Chapter 6
Almost there

Spring 2006

Quiet times passed, marked by evenings when we'd exchange smiles and waves. I was falling in love. She was more than just an average girl next door; she was a national athlete in class XI, an artist at heart, and she seemed to want to connect with me. But did I deserve her? I was scared, you see. I'd never been in love before and was unsure about myself. I was unsettled, wondering if I could make any promises to someone so delicate, so full of potential. I didn't want to hurt her by breaking promises I couldn't keep. I was new to this whole love game.

Then there was Sam, acting all different now. He pretended not to care for her anymore, but it was just a front. It's hard to admit feelings, to say you've lost, especially with pride on the line.

As the cold month of January was winding down, I was riding in a rickshaw during a brisk but pleasant afternoon somewhere in the city. Out of the blue, I saw a familiar face. I spun around to see if it was really her or if my mind was playing tricks on me.

Ami was walking home by herself in her light blue and white school uniform wearing a jacket to beat the wind. She had her familiar red Nike backpack on her shoulders and a radiant expression on her face. She held a half-unwrapped chocolate bar in her hand. She seemed entirely absorbed in her own world, paying little attention to the world and traffic around her. She looked lovely—deriving pure happiness from that chocolate bar.

I signalled the rickshaw driver to stop right away. Within the next two seconds, I leapt off the rickshaw and started walking toward her. It was our first face-to-face meeting, and my nerves were on edge. I couldn't pinpoint what had given me the courage, but my mind was solely focused on a mix of excitement and fear. I had envisioned so many scenarios for our first encounter, but this was unlike any of them. Absolutely random.

As she spotted me, her reaction was a mixture of surprise, joy, and confusion. A broad smile adorned her face, concealing a myriad of emotions beneath. In her excitement, she promptly shoved the remaining chocolate into her mouth, and her cheek puffed up. Silently and swiftly, she tried to finish chewing the bits as we approached each other. I could tell that she was in an equal amount of shock, if not more. My adrenaline surged, much like the first time I saw her outside my window. This was the first time we were going to have a conversation using words.

Suddenly, I noticed Ami looking past me, her gaze fixed on something behind me. Confusion engulfed me as her joyful expressions gave way to sheer panic. I turned around to see what had startled her. It was her father, riding a red motorbike with a matching turban. Although he couldn't have spotted me because I had my back turned towards him, and I wasn't close enough to Ami for him to suspect anyone meeting his highly guarded daughter, it still sent a chill down my spine. At that moment, I wished I were the national athlete instead of her, just in case the need for a quick getaway arose.

Without hesitation and with a quick judgment, I hopped onto another passing auto-rickshaw. By the time I looked back, Ami was already riding pillion with her weightlifter dad.

On my way back to my PG (that's fancy for 'place I stay, Paying Guest'), I couldn't help but wonder if her dad had spotted me. I was legit scared of becoming the next punching bag in his collection. Let me tell you, I was as brave as a kitten in a lion's den. But, secretly, I had a tiny victory dance in my heart. Her smile spilled the beans that day. My brain took a mental selfie of that moment. I can close my eyes, and boom! There she is, going all-in on that chocolate bar, rocking her red backpack with a bottle, and nailing the school uniform look in white and light blue.

For the next few days, I was on high alert. Whenever I spotted her dad, I played detective, trying to decode his facial expressions for any hint of murderous intentions. But his face was a real-life emoji puzzle, and I couldn't crack it. Eventually, I convinced myself that he hadn't spotted me. Even her mom didn't hire an army to increase the security around her daughter.

I attempted the same escapade to catch a glimpse of her again, but it was like searching for a needle in a haystack blindfolded. I didn't even know which school she attended. If I'd asked my landlady about it, she'd have thought I was plotting to contact her, and even Kamal, my buddy, was purposefully clueless about her school info. Her school uniform was the James Bond of outfits—too undercover to reveal her school's identity. Tata had more copycat schools than you could count. So, I locked all my 'life's big mysteries' in my brain vault.

On the flip side, my social life got a boost. PK, Sam, and I became the rooftop cricket champs, or at least we thought we were. Our version of the sport was more like 'miniature cricket' because every time we went for a big hit, the ball decided it preferred the ground over our roof.

My role in the game? Fielder extraordinaire! But let's be real, I wasn't chasing after the ball just for the game's sake. No, sir! My mission was to steal glances at Ami, who stood across on her terrace, giving me 'the look'. She'd stare at me like I was the last slice of pizza, with intermittent checks over her shoulder to ensure her mom was none the wiser.

I had my espionage skills on point to keep her mom and pesky sister out of the loop. Our... whatever-it-was was blossoming like a flower in the Sahara—no future in sight, just many innocent moments.

Chapter 7
Broken Jaw

One evening, Sam returned home after being out somewhere. He had a few folks with him on a couple of motorcycles, and they were making a lot of noise, which I could hear from my window. It was dark, so all I could see were silhouettes. The men on the motorbike and Sam chatted for a bit. When they finally stopped after a chaotic five minutes of muffled, mumbled chat, what we saw when Sam entered the room shook us.

His left cheek was hugely swollen, and his sleeveless shirt was torn and stretched from his neck down his chest. There was blood on his left eyebrow and the corner of his mouth. He looked beaten up, and it was quite a shock. We asked, "What happened to you?" He grumbled, "Please talk quietly," clearly in pain. We urged him to lie down because his face was swelling even more. I sent PK to the market for antiseptic, bandages, and painkillers.

I asked Sam again, "What happened?"

"I don't know, man," he said, tears in his eyes. "I got into a rough situation with about 10-15 guys. I didn't expect it to escalate like this."

As time passed, his face continued to swell. We cleaned his wounds, gave him some glucose and painkillers, and told him to speak when he felt up to it. We were shocked and anxious.

The night was tense. We slept in the same room just to monitor his situation. While taking Sam to the doctor the following day, he shared his story with us. Every bump in the rickshaw made him wince, and he'd add an "Oh" or "Ouch" to his tale.

Sam had gone out to retrieve a cassette he'd left for recording at a shop in the nearby market. (Back then, recording songs on cassette tapes was all the rage.) Normally, whenever we went to the nearby market, we'd go together just for the fun of it or to indulge in some samosas. But if my memory serves me right, this was the first time one of us had ventured out solo.

The shopkeeper at the recording store was inebriated when Sam went to get his cassette back, but that wasn't the root of the problem. The real trouble lay elsewhere. You see, Sam didn't visit that shop just for the recording; he also had an eye on the lady who spent most of her time minding the store there. Sam had a habit of making comments about the lady's, well, assets, with an expression that screamed, "The bigger, the better." Sam had been giving her lingering looks for some time. Poor guy was missing a crucial piece of information: the man sitting at the counter was the lady's husband.

That night, when Sam went to collect his cassette, the husband happened to be around, and unfortunately, he was quite drunk. While Sam asked for his cassette, he couldn't resist gawking at the lady in a way that wasn't very gentlemanly. It turned out that her husband had been keeping an eye on Sam for a few days, and maybe because he was intoxicated, he let loose a barrage of insults, ordering Sam to leave the shop immediately.

For Sam, it evolved into a classic case of a bruised male ego, and his language escalated to a whole new level of nastiness. It didn't take long before things got physical. Sam, being the beefier one, pretty much tossed the tipsy shopkeeper out onto the street. However, what he overlooked was the golden rule of not messing with a local on their own turf. The shopkeeper called for reinforcements, and in a matter of seconds, Sam found himself outnumbered by a dozen angry locals. They were like a swarm of bees, with 10-15 people landing punches on his face. They also called the cops and gave them the lowdown. To make matters worse, the police were firmly on their side, leaving Sam battered and all alone.

"The upper jaw is fractured," the doctor declared after inspecting the X-ray. He held it up at arm's length, squinting at it as if it were some abstract art, and then dropped the bombshell, "You need surgery within two days. We'll have to wire your jaw from the inside and put it back in its place." That clearly explained why Sam's jaw looked more unplugged than an acoustic rock concert.

Up until that moment, Sam had been holding back the real waterworks, clinging to the hope that things would magically work out. But that news broke him like a delicate vase. He wept openly, his hands outstretched, and while the doctor was bewildered by the sudden emotional outburst, we could only imagine the agony he was enduring. He couldn't even eat a bite of solid food and was sentenced to a liquid diet for at least the next two months.

He had a lot of daunting questions to address immediately. What would he tell his parents back home? What to say to the landlady? Where would he have his treatment and surgery? And how on earth was he going to arrange the money for all of this if he wanted to keep it all a secret? It was a real tangled mess. I was the anxious one, but PK was the bold strategist. He came up with a plan.

We decided to tell everyone that Sam had gone to the National Institute of Technology, Tata, to meet a senior and was playing football when a wild shot from someone else smacked him in the face, resulting in a jaw fracture. It was a decent cover story, but stories can't hide all the pain.

We started packing Sam's belongings; he had no reason to stay in Jamshedpur now. He needed to return home for the surgery, which would require delicate care for months afterwards, including that liquid diet ordeal. He was saying goodbye to Tata. A part of me was sad to see the way things were suddenly ending, but another part of me was happy, as I was losing the competitor.

While PK went to get the tickets, I packed up Sam's stuff and tried my best to comfort him. With every word he spoke, tears streamed down his cheeks. He talked about his dreams before coming here, his life's failures, his parents' expectations, and finally, he said something that left me speechless.

"She likes you, dude. She told me herself. I'm sorry I didn't tell you earlier. I was being a real jerk, and I was, well... kind of jealous. But she's a great girl who deserves a guy like you. Reach out to her, hold her hand once, and never let go. And please keep me in the loop about everything else. I hope you'll call me up at home sometimes."

I was at a loss for words. I felt like crap for finding that slice of happiness in his departure. Considering what I knew of him, I grasped that it must have taken a lot for him to express all that, even if he was on painkillers. At that moment, I released any negative feelings I had harboured for him.

It was time, and I hailed an auto-rickshaw. We went to the station to see him off. He attempted to muster a smile, but the physical pain won the battle. That's one of the toughest expressions to witness: when you're trying to smile, but tears stream uncontrollably down your cheeks. We had never anticipated that our time in Tata would throw such challenging days at us and that he would have to leave the city and us under such strange circumstances. Everything happened in a whirlwind; we didn't even have a moment to convey how much we would miss him once he was gone. Despite our friendly competition, we had become so accustomed to having him around. In just a few moments, he was gone, and the weight of our impending longing was palpable in our heavy voices.

Chapter 8
The Ball Game

Suddenly, Sam was no longer part of our small group, and his abrupt absence left a void that weighed on us for a while. However, on the positive side, the chemistry between Ami and me was off the charts. I could feel it intensifying with every passing moment. My confidence and anxiety were on a rollercoaster ride. Both of us had come to realise how much we wanted to talk to each other. On the one hand, I was scared to make a move, but on the other hand, I was becoming aware that time was running out. It was just a matter of a few months; my admission elsewhere would likely mean leaving Tata and perhaps never seeing her again. My fear of her muscular dad, especially after our recent close encounter, and the memory of Sam's swollen face made it tough for me to gather the courage to intercept her on her way back from school. I was a real chicken-hearted guy.

One chilly February morning, she did something different from our usual exchange of smiles. She used hand signals to convey something, much like the last time I had no clue what she meant. It looked like she was throwing something at me, but there was nothing in her hand. She tried a couple more times; every time she crossed my window, she threw something invisible at me, and I was clueless. However, that evening, I mustered the courage to do something bold. I used hand gestures to communicate back and told her that I had started to like her. I made a heart shape with my hands and then pointed to myself and then to her with one hand. I'm not entirely sure if she got it. She was certainly amused by the communication leap I had taken, but if anything, there was frustration on her face. Even though we were naive about most things, one thing was clear: we were pretty terrible at our primary mode of communication, sign language.

The next afternoon, as I left home for the market nearby, an elderly neighbour, speaking in his Punjabi dialect, stopped me with a straightforward question that sent my heart racing.

"Do you have a romantic affair going on, son?"

His question felt like a polite accusation, enough to catch me off guard and terrify me.

"Uh... No, sir! Not at all... But why do you ask?" I was sweating bullets.

"Does anyone else in your group wear glasses?"

I was the only one of the three of us living there who wore glasses. The way he narrowed down on me with whatever he implied made me fear a potential confrontation with her father in the near future.

"No, sir," I stammered, "only me, but why do you ask?" These were strange and seemingly irrelevant questions. But what did glasses have to do with anything?

"Hmm, I received a letter delivered to my home, and I'm pretty sure it was meant for someone much younger." His gaze was intense and uncomfortable.

"Oh! It must have been a mistake by the postman, Uncle. I can pick it up now or from your house on my way back." I was relieved to hear that it was just a wrongly delivered letter. However, his response made my heart race like a thousand horses galloping inside my chest.

"No, no, son! It didn't come by post; it came by a BALL."

"What?" Now, the old man was getting even more mysterious, and my curiosity was reaching its peak. If he knew about it, and judging by how everyone in the neighbourhood was looking at me that day, I assumed everyone must know, and I was almost certain I was in line for a beating from her father. My landlady had warned me that her father's hand was as heavy as a rock, and the guy who lived here before me couldn't even stand for days after facing his punches and kicks. I had recently witnessed someone getting thrashed, and the thought of having swollen cheeks and a disfigured jaw was the icing on the cake. I was trying hard to act like everything was normal, but I had never been so scared in my life until that moment.

"Can I see the letter, uncle?" I asked, my legs still trembling.

"Oh, yes, you can see it, but I'm not going to give it to you." Man, he was a sly old fellow. I wasn't sure why he was keeping the letter to himself, but the most likely reason seemed to be to show it to Ami's father. Some people are like that. Sadists.

"It's fine; if it's for me, I just want to see it." I wished I could act all cool and bogart-like, but all I could manage was pretending to be innocent!

The letter went like this:

To the guy in glasses, I know we both want to talk to each other, but communicating through our eyes and signals is getting hard. I think we should meet up. I was hoping you would approach me first, but the way you ran off that day after seeing my dad, you might never do it. So, could you pass me your mobile number? Your friend.

The very obvious and frightening question came next, "How deeply are you involved?" I responded hurriedly, "Do you really think I am involved? Do I look like I am? I'm here for my studies and nothing else, Sir. It's okay if you want to keep the letter, but so that you know, I'm not up to anything wrong. Thank you."

Gosh, I was as nervous as a long-tailed cat in a room full of rocking chairs. I was on the defensive. What if her dad discovered this letter, or, heaven forbid, what if he was already in the loop?

A weird shiver ran down my spine. I did my best to play the naive card.

"But, uncle, can I at least have the ball?" He shot me a peculiar look, paused for a beat, scratched his head, and finally surrendered it.

So, there I was, holding the ball, the very one she probably used to wrap the letter and chuck toward my roof. Unfortunately, it decided to take a detour and land in the hands of my lovely neighbour, the resident fun-killer! If I had a dictionary of colourful words, I would've probably flipped through it to find the perfect description for him.

That evening, she looked at me with bated breath, waiting for a response. Little did she know the adventurous journey her letter had undertaken. After that, I abandoned my rooftop escapades, but I couldn't resist peeping out of my window. I'd briefed PK on all the juicy details, so he was also on high alert, scanning for anything odd around her house or among her family members.

Chapter 9
To be or not to be

Nearly two weeks passed without any progress since her attempt to pass that letter to me. I had no idea why her dad, famous for his 'thrashings,' had spared me. Maybe my neighbour liked my innocent appearance, or perhaps he felt some sympathy and didn't spill the beans on her father.

Things were becoming excruciatingly painful. I would gaze at her from my window, unable to bear those sad, expectant eyes. The poor girl had no clue what had happened to her letter. I couldn't bring myself to go to the roof and stare at her endlessly anymore.

The two-week silence had intensified the confusion and fear already rooted within me. I was afraid of not being the guy she deserved. Knowing myself well—my fears and quirks—I acknowledged I wasn't a hero or a macho movie star we all admire and aspire to be like. That silent love had given me a different perspective. I wondered if I could promise her a lifetime commitment and what would happen if I couldn't fulfil it. I was just a student, doing nothing more than preparing for an engineering college entrance exam. I had heard of such love stories but wasn't sure if they ever had happy endings. I was going away from the place in a couple of months.

I talked to PK about her.

"I think I like her," I confessed.

He listened patiently as I poured out all my confusion and fears. It felt good to have someone who understood where I was coming from.

"I love her, but I can't promise her anything," I said. "She's so naive, and I don't want to play with her life. She's unspoiled and young, probably experiencing her first real crush. I don't want to build her dreams only to shatter them later. I don't think she'll end up with me. In a few months, we will be in some engineering college and gone. It's been three seasons of knowing each other, and we still haven't talked to each other. Where do you think we will end up?"

PK understood.

He looked at me and then out the window into the darkness, comprehending everything but unsure of what to make of it all. He thought it was a pretty heavy situation and admitted he had never thought about anything like that before. "She also loves you, I know that," was all he could say.

"I know that too! And that's what's tearing me apart! She doesn't even know me. She's not falling in love with me; she's falling in love with an idea, a version of me that she has in her mind. The day she truly knows me, she might walk away. I have nothing to offer her! I am just a guy from the village, and I am seeing these things for the first time. People in love go on bike rides and eat in restaurants. I don't even have a motorbike, and I don't even know how to ride one. I won't be able to take her to nice places; she won't be able to introduce me to her friends. Oh! This is so confusing..."

"I don't know what to tell you," PK responded, his voice filled with understanding. "Follow what your heart says; if it's written in your fate, you won't be a loser."

He paused, gave me an affirming look regarding his words, and added, "Why don't you tell her all this? Maybe she'll understand. And you won't have to carry any guilt because you've been honest with her."

Yes, that actually made a lot of sense!

Chapter 10
The Number Game

Days of internal struggle had left my heart and mind in a state of utter confusion. I was bamboozled, and the impending engineering entrance exams only added to my woes.

As I would sit at my desk, surrounded by a fortress of textbooks and notes, my mind would drift literally along with my eyes to outside the window, and the world of numbers and laws would fade into the background. I was torn, caught in a tempest of the heart and mind. On one end, there was the future my parents envisioned for me, shaped by their sacrifices and hopes. And on the other was her. She was the melody in my life that made my heart sing, the vibrant splash of colour in a world that often felt monochrome otherwise. When my world was all about her, time would stop, and the worries about differential equations and thermodynamics would melt away.

The journey ahead was uncertain, but I knew that these choices would shape not just my career but the very essence of who I was and who I would become.

PK kept pushing me to follow my heart's desire. What I had initially thought about not messing with Ami's life was starting to make a lot of sense, or at least that's what I believed at the time.

So, I did something utterly unthinkable; I started avoiding her. I didn't want to encourage her feelings, as I didn't want her

to fall apart once she got to know me better or, perhaps, after I had left that place. In truth, I was trying to shield myself from the possibility of falling apart as well. And just to put things in context, all of this was happening before we even got together.

Even though it was incredibly difficult for me, I felt compelled to do it. At that very moment, I began to feel like a grown-up, filled with philosophical ideas and moral sides to take. I didn't want to play with her emotions because, frankly, I didn't have my own life figured out at that point. I firmly believe that a promise made should be a promise kept, and in matters of love, we should never break our promises. Maybe it was love, a kind of love that, at that moment, was preventing me from loving her the way I truly wanted to. It was my first love, and it happened with a girl I had never talked to for the first 10 months of our life, and we knew each other.

I tried too hard for too long, and it had been almost two weeks of me ignoring her. Guilt was brewing inside me like fresh breakfast coffee. To escape the situation, I began spending my evenings out because coming home meant facing her expectant eyes. Even she had stopped waving. Instead, she'd just stroll past my window, peering at my uninterested face with a look that said, 'What happened? I have no clue what happened since I threw the ball to you.' It was as if she'd lost something she never really had. I had no answers, no explanations to offer, and no relief for her or me.

I couldn't figure out how to convey my thoughts to her. Sometimes, I'd turn off my room lights to avoid her gaze, but I couldn't resist peeking out to watch her walk by, occasionally glancing at my darkened room.

The silence was driving me nuts. Over the past ten months, we'd grown so used to communicating through smiles—only smiles—that we never felt the rush to declare our love. It was just understood between us. I felt a pang of sadness about my recent actions but was firmly convinced that it was the right thing to do. I couldn't take the risk of hurting her or making promises I couldn't keep. She was suffering needlessly, and I was a big part of that suffering. I wanted to explain my perspective to her, to tell her why I was behaving like this all of a sudden.

Enough was enough! I told myself, "She must know how I feel," and I meant every word of it. That evening, I went to my terrace, determined to let her in on my emotions. I tried to gesture to her for her phone number, doing a little pretend-phone dance. She was taken aback at first and froze like a deer in headlights. But then, she composed herself and started communicating something with her fingers. It was too far, and her fingers were too tiny to see, so it didn't work out.

Realising that I was probably misinterpreting her, I abandoned that idea and instead decided to give her my number. She gestured that she was also coming to her roof. Fate smiled upon us that day; her mom and sister were out shopping, and her father was nowhere in sight. No spies to worry about.

We stood facing each other on our respective roofs, at the farthest ends, ensuring that no one from the street could catch a glimpse of us. PK sat by the window in my room, ready to dash to my rescue if any danger loomed. She held a pen and probably picked it up on her way to the roof. In her lovely maroon-black dress with her hair blowing with the wind, she looked as peaceful as a morning song—an angel. The ageing sun was on its way to hide behind the houses on her side of the street, but that evening, in the soft twilight, she shimmered. She seemed more mine than ever.

I had never experienced love before; I had no idea how it felt. There was a sparkle in her eyes, and the street below was quiet. The timing was perfect. Even today, when I close my eyes and reminisce about that magical moment, I can hear the faint tinkling of the wind chime in her garden. Everything feels just right, intact. I can recall every detail of that evening, even the scent of the air and the caress of the breeze.

I started trying to give her my phone number using hand signals. The distance between us made it a bit tricky, and I kept wiggling my fingers for a while. But when it became clear that my finger dance wasn't working, I decided to go with my brilliant plan B.

I rushed downstairs, raided my room for a stack of newspapers, and got to work. I cut out the digits I needed in big, bold letters and proudly displayed the numbers 9834387070 in sequence. It took me a good half-hour to show her all nine digits, but when I was done, her face lit up like a firecracker. You could see the joy in her big, beaming smile; she looked like a happy rabbit.

We stood there, staring at each other, lost in our own little world, for what felt like forever. Then she made a hand gesture that basically said, "Get down from the roof right now!" She moved her hand in a circle from the top to the bottom and formed a little roof with her palm. It was crystal clear—she wanted me to hightail it downstairs. Her small gestures like this always kept me out of the neighbourhood gossip mill, especially in front of her tough-as-nails dad.

I heeded her signal, and I was head over heels in love, floating on cloud nine.

Chapter 11
A macho oopsie

A whole day had passed, and still, no call. Quite surprising, I must say! I remember the anxiety building up inside me as the noon sun blazed. I couldn't help but wonder why she hadn't called yet. In the back of my mind, I started concocting possible explanations. Maybe she had the wrong number? What if the number got somehow nabbed by her parents? My earlier urgency to talk to her and share my fears and insecurities had somehow morphed into something else. The previous day, when we were both on the rooftop, just looking at her face had given me such an innocent, satisfying feeling that why I needed to speak to her had taken a backseat... my heart had taken the wheel.

As the evening rolled in, around five o'clock, I couldn't spot her on the street or in her little front garden. I didn't panic too much because... she was on the phone with me.

"Hello?"

"Who's this?" I asked, even though it was pretty obvious who it was. But I liked the idea of pretending not to know.

"Ghoooooooooost!" she replied, pausing for a moment. "Did I actually scare you?" Her question was genuine. "Who else could it be? How many girls have you given your number to?"

"Oh, Ami?" I made a half-hearted attempt to hide the excitement and happiness bubbling up inside me, but I'm sure it was still pretty evident in my voice.

"No, silly, a ghost." She sounded sweet. Very sweet! She had the innocence of a child in her voice. This was the first time I heard her voice so clearly. I was talking to her.

"Is this your number?"

"No, and listen, I'm calling from a phone booth. I'm at the cyber café for the next hour. Come here as soon as you can."

"Which cyber café?"

"How many cyber cafés do you think we have in this market, Mr. Bookworm?" She was so informal and confident. It was like she'd known me for ages. And, yes, there was only one cyber café in the neighbourhood.

"Bookworm! Why?"

"Because I've always seen you sitting at your table, by your books."

"No, it's not like that. In fact, you should be called Miss Bookworm. I always see you strolling in your little garden with a book in your hands, but your eyes aren't on them."

"Oh, then what should I call you? Mr. Table Lamp?"

And then, the most beautiful laughter I'd ever heard in my life filled my ears.

"Listen, come fast. My mom isn't here right now, but she'll be back in an hour."

"What if she comes back early?"

"Then my dad will give you a good thrashing, and I'll be locked in a room for a few days."

This was more information than I had bargained for. Why did it seem like every sweet girl on this planet had a formidable father? I'd seen it in movies a lot, but this was getting a bit too real.

Until the day before, my plan had been straightforward: tell her I wasn't ready for any emotional relationship. But after that conversation, my resolve began to waver even more. There was no denying it; I was head over heels in love. We already had an emotional bond. Just one day without seeing her made me feel like I was missing a piece of myself, and I could see the same anxiety on her face when we reunited.

She was my lucky charm. At that moment, I found myself daydreaming about all the wonderful things I wanted to say to her and imagining how having a face-to-face conversation for the first time would feel. We exchanged glances, smiles, and waves, and now, after almost ten months, we were about to have a real conversation. My excitement was like a kid on his birthday morning.

However, a sudden thought struck me: Was this truly what I wanted? I paused momentarily, and every thought in my head stood at a standstill. Clarity emerged. My inner philosopher resurfaced. I took a deep breath, scrutinised my true intentions for this meeting, engaged in a somewhat childish and innocent internal struggle with my emotions (as I would now call it), and finally, I knew what I had to do.

Within five minutes, I rushed out without even changing my shirt or bothering with deodorant. Time was of the essence, and I didn't have the luxury to shave. And, as per the decision of my righteous self, a clean shave wasn't deemed necessary. It was challenging, as a stubborn inner voice kept insisting, 'You love her; you have to do it.'

My adrenaline surged as if I had consumed a few too many energy drinks. PK and I walked toward the bustling market, puffing away on cigarettes. My heart felt like it had entered the Grand Prix race. The cyber café sat at the tip of one of the three branches of this 'Y'-shaped marketplace. To play it safe, I sent PK in first to check if Ami was inside. Meanwhile, I attempted to appear casual, a challenging feat given the whirlwind of emotions—excitement, fear, and a touch of philosophy.

PK took a peek inside the café and shook his head, signalling a 'no, she's not here.' I was struck dumb, my heart pounding as if it had a personal vendetta against me. But as I scanned the area, I spotted her standing by a ladies' tailor shop nearby, narrowly averting an impending heart attack. She looked at me, smiled, and met my guilt-driven, I can't do this, self-righteous, subdued smile. I had never felt so out of place in my life. She was clearly very confused.

I instructed PK to position himself outside the café at the central junction of the 'Y'-shaped road. His mission was simple: alert me if her mom was heading our way from any direction.

Inside the café, I was a bundle of nerves, like a child on stage for the very first time, despite months of rehearsal. I was physically next to her but couldn't even look at her. Having studied in an all-boys school with no sisters in my family tree, this was my maiden face-to-face encounter with a girl. Smiles and waves had been safe, but in the flesh, I felt clueless about how to behave, what to talk about, or how to start a conversation.

The café bustled with people, and every chair was taken. Without a second thought, I settled into the only available seat while she remained standing behind me. An awkward silence enveloped us, and for the next few tense minutes, we exchanged nothing. I felt her presence behind me, her uneven breath adding to the palpable tension. My legs trembled, seemingly possessed by a will of their own. With each passing moment, I dreaded the arrival of her mother. What a loss for a story's beginning.

When a chair became vacant, she seized the opportunity, pulling it closer to sit beside me. Sensing my nervousness, she attempted to ease the tension. I still couldn't bring myself to look directly at her, stealing only occasional glances from the corner of my eyes. She wore a hot pink half-sleeved shirt paired with faded light blue jeans. Excess Talcum powder sported around her neck, and her hair was tightly pulled back into a ponytail. Her lips sported a touch of lipstick, and intricate mehndi designs adorned her delicate hands up to her elbows. However, her nails were only half-painted. Her naturally curled eyelashes, accentuated by black eyeliner, framed eyes filled with unspoken words. At any other moment, I might have lost myself in the sheer loveliness of her innocence or burst into laughter at her unique fashion sense, but my nervousness prevailed.

"Aren't you going to say anything?" She broke the ice, removed her hair band, and released her voluminous curly hair from its ponytail.

"Not m...much," I stammered out, surprising even myself. My voice trembled, and she seemed too good to be true.

"Really?" she inquired.

I wasn't sure if she took it as an insult or understood my nervousness, but she was visibly taken aback. Perhaps she hadn't anticipated such a response after months of silent but evident affection.

"Nothing much if you don't have anything to talk about," she said with a hint of disappointment. "I thought we'd talked enough through smiles, and it was about time we had a real conversation."

Summoning all my courage, I spoke again, "Actually... sorry, I shouldn't have done this," my tone shifted dramatically. The slim chance of salvaging a friendly chat, still visible in her eyes, vanished. She looked bewildered and likely hurt. The more I tried to act normal, the more my nervousness held me hostage. I practically blew it up.

"I ha...I hav...I have a girlfriend already, and I am sure.. curious about her," I babbled, not fully comprehending my words. But the way I stuttered, I'm sure she realised I was lying to avoid her. Tears welled up in her eyes, and despite her efforts to hold them back, the look in her eyes spoke volumes. It was an emotional-chemical reaction I hadn't anticipated. For months, we had built a close connection without uttering a word, silently affirming our love for each other.

Attempting to divert the conversation, she said, "I don't like you smoking," her voice heavy with emotion, and holding back tears became increasingly difficult for her.

"I'm sorry; I'm a chain smoker," I replied, not sure what had come over me. As I had already started distancing myself from her, I was now more determined, trying to give her every reason to dislike me as much as possible. It was the most nerve-wracking moment of my life, and it felt like I was possessed.

"Wouldn't you quit, even if I asked you to?"

She looked directly into my eyes, and I turned mine to the computer screen. I didn't have the courage to lie to those simple eyes. "My girlfriend has asked me a hundred times, but I never quit." I lied rudely.

She fell silent, and I could sense that each new statement was another blow to her.

"What are your future plans?" I tried to keep the conversation going because, deep down, I felt like this might be the last time we spoke.

"I want to fly. I want to be an air hostess."

"That sounds great; I hope you achieve it."

She was catching on to the fact that I was just trying to make small talk. She tried to hold back, but it became too much for her.

"Why did you do all that when you had to say this to me?" A tiny tear rolled down from the corner of her eye as she tightly shut them for a couple of seconds.

I had no answer. I was feeling guilty, and rightfully so. I had never been with a girl like this, never faced a girl crying, and there I was with no idea of what to do next.

"We can be friends... good friends."

"When are you going away?" she asked straight away, not beating around the bush.

"In a month."

Her silence made me more uncomfortable than her words. I was still incredibly nervous, and my legs were shaking – literally. I couldn't bear the guilt any longer. I decided it was time to be completely honest with her, hoping she would understand.

"Can I tell you something?"

She didn't say a word, just kept her head bent.

"I don't have any girlfriend I told you about. In fact, I've never had a girlfriend, you know what I mean, don't you? I'm a very introverted guy. Leave alone, girls; I've even been afraid of talking to guys I don't know. You entered my life like an angel, and you'll probably never know how much you've changed me. And yes, I also like you; I like you a lot. But I believe I'm not the guy you deserve, and also, there is no future for us as of now. You deserve someone very nice, tough, and macho. I know it surprises you to hear me stammering right now, but I don't stammer this much; it's just because I'm nervous. I've just been trying to get into a good engineering college for an year now. I don't know if I'll ever get into one. I come from a very small place, and I don't know what lies before me."

I really had no idea what I was blurting out in front of her. All this time, she was looking at her hands, which she held together since she had come to sit next to me. I noticed she had crossed her first two fingers. Her fingers were slender and clenched together. She looked lovely. I wished I could hold her in my arms, but I couldn't gather the courage to do so. I continued...

"In a month, I will be out of this place. You will be alone. Maybe someone else will enter your life then, someone who is much better than me, someone who you deserve. Maybe I will fall for someone in my college or wherever I go. I don't know what college I am going to get into; I don't know what my job will be. I can't make promises; I am not in a position to."

I could hear her sobbing, a feeble, broken, heavy breathing. In her eyes, the next teardrop was forming and ready to glide down her cheek at any moment.

"Don't cry, please. I have never been with a girl like this, leaving aside one crying. I don't know what else to tell you." It was so new for me. I felt like holding her tight in my arms so intensely, hugging and comforting her, but I didn't know how people did that. Instead, I gathered all my courage and took her hands, holding them tight. Her hands were warm and soft, like smooth satin between my palms.

"Now, if someday, after two years, you still have this feeling alive, I will be there for you. I promise. As of now, we probably can't even be friends. I have my exams coming up, and I can't distract myself. Moreover, I believe in love; these are not false promises, and I am not in a position to promise you anything right now. I seriously hope you understand."

Whatever she was going through, I was going through the same. She just nodded her head.

"Will you fill out my online slam book if you don't mind?" I had a page on Yahoo Geocities at that time where I had a page specially made for a slam book. I looked at her, and our eyes held almost the same emotions.

She took the keyboard with her trembling hands; she was shaken just the same.

"Okay, let me type for you," and she kept on answering the questions I asked her.

Name: Ahmanpreet Gill Date of Birth: 18/10/88 Nickname: She looked at me, "Whatever you would like to call me." Nickname: Barbie (I filled it in myself) And it went on...

"On the 17th of this month, I have my annual festival at school. I will wait for you by the gate."

"I won't be coming, Ami. I am sorry..." Even before I could finish my answer, she got up to leave. She turned back to look at me once and said, "You don't feel anything, do you?" and she left.

She went away with a heavy heart. I was sad, too. Wondering what she meant by her last sentence, I got up, paid the cyber café guy, and took a deep puff, snatching the cigarette from PK's hand.

"Did I do right, PK?"

"No," it was a straightforward answer. Not surprising to me. He always wanted me to go for her. Though he also had notions like I was not ready for commitment or anything, I don't know why that evening he seemed more irritated with me than ever, maybe because he saw her going back with tears in her eyes.

I called Sam for support. I knew he would appreciate that, for whatever reasons he wishes to associate with it. But everyone suddenly became my furious cupid that evening; even he didn't like it. "Dude, if you had to break her heart like this, why did you reciprocate her feelings in the first place?" Sam was really angry.

I had no answers. How could I have told them that I had already started feeling stupid for what I had done, but I had to defend myself since I had already done that? I was too convinced that I did the right thing because I was going to go away; distancing myself from her was better than breaking her heart. Fear and confusion had brainwashed me.

I took a new SIM card for my phone and changed my number so that she could not contact me anymore. I was on fire!

Chapter 12
Winds of Change

Two weeks later, I returned from Kolkata after appearing in my entrance exam for Manipal Institute of Technology. The test went well, and I was confident about clearing it. I was never such an ambitious student to consider only IITs or nothing. It felt good to have completed the preparations after a year of hard work.

PK, upon hearing about how the exam went, congratulated me. Detecting a hint of sadness in PK's words, I realised the time had come for me to leave Tata, for both of us. Soon, he'd also have a good exam like this, which is how the ball should roll. My purpose there had been fulfilled, which meant no more hanging out with friends, no more Street Number 12, no more Punjabi colony, and, most importantly, no more Ami.

Time is a peculiar thing. When you're happy, it seems to fly unnoticed, but when you're sad, it drags on, almost standing still. The impending change weighed heavily on my heart, irrespective of whether it was for the better or worse.

Despite the sense of accomplishment from my exams, the thought of leaving Tata weighed on me like a heavy stone in my gut. I sat by my window, staring out at the street. There she was, standing at the front gate of her house, wearing a purple t-shirt and white shorts. She looked as cute as ever, but her face bore an unmistakable gloom. Even a fool could read it – she had a feeling

I was leaving. I shared the same realisation that everything was coming to an end soon. Time flies by.

Certain thoughts began to trouble me, mainly due to their controversial and risky nature. Suddenly, I felt an overwhelming desire to talk to her. I made a decision that I knew would change my life forever. I signalled for her to call me.

Oops! She didn't have my new number. Just two weeks ago, the righteous me had changed it after our episode at the cyber cafe. Upon inserting my old SIM card, my phone proudly displayed that the previous line was no longer in service. I needed to give her my new number right away, but how? The last time I gave her my number was a stroke of luck, as her family happened to be out. Getting lucky twice would have been a divine intervention, and I couldn't rely on that. So, I had to come up with a different plan.

In the afternoon, I visited her school, as she had mentioned during our last meeting. However, when I realised it was a girls-only convent school, I couldn't muster the courage to stand outside the entrance gate because, on some random days, her dad would pick her up from school instead of the auto-rickshaw. I waited for her at the next intersection, hoping she would pass by, but no luck. The 15th of the month reminded me that her school fest was on the 17th. Everything was unfolding like a fast-forwarded slapstick comedy sequence, and I couldn't contain my restlessness to meet her.

16th April 02 (Diary) - The Next Day

Woke up early, determined to find a way to contact her. Changing my number now felt like the stupidest thing I had ever done. I decided to follow her auto in the morning to learn her route to school. My plan is to catch her somewhere along the way to give her my new number. Waiting in front of her school after her classes ended was risky, as her father might show up and see me. Nevertheless, I tried that yesterday.

In the afternoon, I positioned myself at the turn in the road near her convent, but I couldn't spot her. I am at a loss about how to give her my new number. In the evening, she was standing by her gate, still wearing the same sad expression in her eyes. When I signalled her from the rooftop two days ago to call me, I think she may have tried my old number and failed. PK and I are both clueless about how to get her the new number. Every time I try to communicate with her, her mom is around. The brief moment I had today was wasted because I tried to tell her too many things at once, and it wasn't enough time to give her the new number. I feel sorry for her, as I hurt her in our first meeting. Now that I want to connect again with her before leaving this place for good, God, please help me. Please... I'm running out of options.

17th April 02 (Diary): Day of the annual festival at her school.

Today was a sad and eventful day. In the morning, I followed her rickshaw to the second turn of our street and saw it stop at a house on the next street. She was inside while the auto driver stepped out to call another girl for carpooling. She could see me, which made me happy, but I had a feeling her mom was following me. Her mom is starting to catch on. For the last two days, she has seen me leave home at the same time her daughter's rickshaw departs. Although I'm not scared anymore, I don't want to create a scene in the colony before I leave. Besides, we were not far from home, just on a different street in the colony. I couldn't reach out to her. She gazed at me, and I made some odd gestures, trying to convey that I'd meet her in the same place that afternoon and visit her school at night as she had asked, but not sure if she understood.

I waited again in the afternoon after her school ended, but her auto didn't pass that way. When I returned home, I saw that she was already home. In the evening, PK and I went to her school. They had the annual fest going on, and I could hear music and a lot of people inside as well as outside. But it was a futile endeavour for us. We didn't have a pass to go inside. There was a security guard with a thick moustache giving PK, and me looks; as we didn't look like parents, we didn't look like students of that girls' school either! Ami had mentioned that she'd wait for me by the entrance. PK and I hovered around the entrance gate for almost three hours inconspicuously before it started getting suspicious.

We didn't see Ami. PK was disappointed and a bit irritated with me, as he needed to study for his exams (he still needed to crack one to get into a good school). However, I know he'll be fine in a day; he never holds on to such feelings. All this waiting was exhausting, and fear was creeping inside me, slowly starting to take over. Fear that I'll have to leave Jamshedpur without telling her how I feel about her right now. I feel stupid for my foolishness during our last meeting. What was I thinking? I wish I could make her a promise. God, please help.

And so, those two anxious days passed, with the weekend featuring a constant humming of the Backstreet Boys song, 'Quit Playing Games with My Heart.'

Monday - Morning

I found myself back in the next lane to mine, the same spot where I had seen her auto-rickshaw stop the previous day. I patiently waited for her rickshaw to halt once again, this time to pick up the other girl who lived there. It was a fact I had only discovered last week, and I couldn't help but feel a tinge of shame for spending almost 11 months in the area without knowing this seemingly small but crucial detail. Nevertheless, I had a plan for that morning.

Executing my genius plan, PK stationed himself at the first bend of my street, strategically positioned to keep an eye on me. We had devised a signal in case her mother decided to make an appearance and track my movements.

When the auto finally stopped, I hastily stubbed out my cigarette and hurried toward her. I handed her my new number on a crumpled piece of paper and informed her that I wanted to talk. Glancing at PK, I saw no sign of her mom approaching, which brought a wave of relief.

In response to my friendly approach, Ami surprised me with her reply, saying, "I don't want to impose any boundaries on you. I know you're sincere at heart and don't need to explain it to me again. All I want is for you to be my best friend forever and return this slam book after filling it up at the same place tomorrow morning." Her words sent a shiver down my spine. I couldn't help but question the term "best friends," a phrase girl often used for short-term or seasonal friends to create a sense of significance. I suddenly felt more foolish about my behaviour during our first meeting. Best friends? Huh!

Despite my desire to explain my newfound affection for her, my male ego, a source of trouble in the past, resurfaced. After all, during our last encounter, I had explicitly mentioned that I wasn't ready for any relationship. How could I now kneel before her and make a romantic confession?

I smiled at her, ensuring she could see a hint of something positively ambiguous in my eyes. Time was of the essence, and the risk of someone witnessing our conversation was high in the small colony. She caught the twinkle in my eye and seemed enchanted. My mission was accomplished, and I received a signal from PK that her mom was approaching. As anticipated, my suspicions about her mother were not unfounded. I hurried away, and PK, my trusty accomplice, vanished in a different direction.

CHAPTER 13
A LOT CAN HAPPEN OVER COFFEE

On that same day at 9 a.m., armed with an assortment of colourful pens I had purchased that morning for this purpose, I embarked on the delightful task of filling out her crimson Slam book. It had heart-shaped patterns, a solitary blemish, and a deliberate scratch obscuring the printed price.

Seated comfortably to complete my own section on the middle page, I followed the unspoken Slam book etiquette, which held that the first, last, and middle pages were the most coveted. Unfortunately, the first page was claimed by her sister, and she herself had filled the final page, leaving me with the middle one. Nonetheless, everything I learned about her from perusing her slam book entry brought a smile to my face. I got to know about all the other people in her life, all her friends, and how and what they think about her.

Here's how I filled in her Slam book:

Name: Nav

Birthday: January 20th, 1988 (though technically, I was born at midnight—the perfect hour for the arrival of ghosts)

Nickname: Call me whatever you like.

Address: Why? Planning to visit? You'll get it when the day comes.

Contact: Give me a call; I gave you my number this morning.

Books I like: Cosmopolitan.

Music: Pink Floyd, The Beatles, Poison, Bryan Adams... actually, the list is quite long.

Best Friends: Sunny, PK, Andy, Sam, Suniti, and you.

Best Teachers: Mr. Amitabh Roy Sharma and Mr. B. J. Rodrigues.

Hobbies: Sitting by my window and watching the cutest girl around, playing down in the street, writing poems, listening to music, and reading books.

Mouthwatering Dishes: Anything prepared by my mom, especially her flying dish (he he).

Idea of a First Date: At the Cape of Good Hope.

Describe Yourself:

I am the tiger's empty cage. I am the mystery's final page.

I am a stranger's lovely glance. I am the hero's only chance.

I am the Christmas morning toy. I am the gin in the gin-soaked boy. f

Lines for Me:

I will be there for you, wait for me, come to me. I feel the same for you as you feel for me. You know it.

Looking back on it now, I can't help but relive that fresh feeling—the fragrance of those pages meticulously adorned with hearts over every 'i' using coloured pens. How naive life was. Everything I wrote was my best attempt to create an impression, spanning from English musicians I had ever heard of to the poor jokes that I can't laugh at today. Falling in love truly is an incredible sensation.

At 11 a.m., a peculiar phone call reached me.

"Hello, Mr. Table Lamp," she began, her voice melodic.

"Ah! Hi, Ami," I responded, my words accompanied by an awkward stammer that prompted her polite laughter. It seemed that I couldn't escape my tendency to stammer whenever I spoke to her.

"Leave whatever you're doing and come to the School of Hope. Right now!" she urged.

"School of Hope?" I queried.

"Yes, sir, the School of Hope. Haven't you heard of it?" she retorted.

"What is it? Where is it?" I inquired, intrigued.

"It's a school for differently-abled kids. Ask the rickshaw driver?" she teased.

"Hmmm... When did they transfer you from the Convent to that? Well, whenever it happens, I'm happy about it. You seem to fit right in," I replied, attempting to maintain a casual and familiar tone. Inside, I couldn't help but smile at my own efforts.

She chuckled in response. "Ha. Ha. Ha. Very funny. Happy? See, I even laughed at your joke. Now come here; I don't have much time. I'm at the phone booth near the entrance."

"Okay, I'm coming," I agreed.

"You'd better hurry up, or I'm going back to my school," she warned playfully.

A sweet laughter followed her warning. The way she talked to me always surprised me, as if she had known me for a long time!

Although it was already close to noon, I hadn't even brushed my teeth, let alone shaved. Time was running out, and she hadn't given me a chance to prepare properly. Grabbing my wallet, which held barely 100 bucks, I left my appearance as dishevelled as it had been when I first met her. It wasn't entirely my fault; she simply hadn't allowed me the luxury of preparation. Nonetheless, I managed to reach the School of Hope within 15 minutes.

She stood before me, wearing a knee-length frock instead of her usual school uniform. I had no idea how she had managed to change her attire so quickly, considering I had seen her go off to school earlier in the morning. Regardless, there she was, smiling at me, and I couldn't help but smile back.

"Shall we walk?" she suggested.

"I don't know. Where are we going?" I replied, attempting to act cool while my heart raced. This was the closest I had ever walked with a girl other than the unknown faces at movie theatre entrances. Nervousness crept over me, and I tried my best to appear composed.

"Somewhere quiet, where my dad can't see you, and you won't lose any of your teeth. You have all 32, don't you?" she inquired, but what bothered me was how frequently she brought up her father in our conversations. I couldn't help but feel a sense of fear whenever she mentioned him. She seemed oblivious to the anxiety she was causing in me.

"Well, the word 'teeth' reminds me that I haven't brushed today, so keep your distance – statutory warning," I joked, attempting to divert the conversation.

She giggled.

"Where were you on the night of your school festival? I was waiting for you at the gate for over three hours." I asked her.

"You were? Don't lie to me, mister. I was waiting for you at the entrance," she retorted. "Let me tell you, I'm very angry with you for that. I really wish you had come that day. I had already told all my friends about you."

"But I told you during our first meeting that I wouldn't be coming. Why are you angry with me?" I inquired.

"Then why did you come, Mr. Tube light?" she said with a triumphant tone.

I had no answer, and she continued to tease me. "In the evenings, when you play cricket, you wear a cap even when it's cloudy, and now, when it's so sunny, you came without it? Where did you leave your brains, Mr. Tube light?"

"I forgot it in my haste," I admitted, amused by her playful jabs. Although I had considered various nicknames for her, like Miss Woodpecker (for her non-stop chatter) or Miss Stick Insect (for her slender frame), I had stuck with calling her Barbie or Ami. After all, it was only our first meeting, and I wasn't accustomed to using those names yet.

We continued walking through the empty, wide roads of one of the posh areas of Jamshedpur. There was hardly anyone around, and the weather was pleasant. I had no idea why she thought it was so sunny. She walked very close to me, and our hands brushed against each other several times, sometimes accidentally and sometimes intentionally, as if we both sought an excuse for the contact. I still remember the wide, open roads, the trees casting random patterns of shadows, the sky with light blue clouds, and the sensation of first love. I wished the road would stretch on forever.

"Where are we going, madam?" I asked again, sensing that the road was nearing its end and we were about to enter a bustling market area.

"How about CCD?" she suggested.

CCD, Café Coffee Day! I had never been to a CCD before, but I had a notion that it was quite an expensive place. I hadn't frequented many such establishments before, and the word on the street was that girls often leaned toward pricier options. What concerned me even more was the meagre hundred bucks in my wallet when I left home, and I had already paid for the rickshaw ride.

"Can't we go somewhere else?" I attempted to change the venue, hoping to sidestep any financial embarrassment. I didn't even know what they served there, apart from coffee, as the name suggested. I berated myself for not borrowing some cash from PK before coming.

"Why? Don't you like coffee, or can't you sit in the air conditioning?" she inquired.

"No, it's okay," I conceded. Despite my words, I couldn't shake the uncomfortable feeling inside me. What if the bill arrived, and I had to ask her to pay on our first proper meeting?

"Which room is yours in your house?" I momentarily changed the topic, eager to steer clear of any financial discussions. I noticed a smile on her face each time I spoke, perhaps because of my occasional stammering.

"The one at the front. But why do you ask? You wouldn't be allowed into my room anyway," she replied, a mischievous look in her eyes. I couldn't explain why, but I found her silly jokes rather endearing.

"Oh, the garage?" I teased.

"No, Mr. Tube light, not the garage. The garage is where my

dad keeps guys who hit on me, all tied up, hungry, and helpless," she said dramatically, "and occasionally, they get a beating."

I chuckled at her playful joke but grew nervous again as we approached the crowded area. What if someone spotted us and reported back to her family?

"How was your exam?" she inquired. She knew my exams were ongoing, and whenever I was away from Tata for a few days, she could tell that I was gone somewhere to write an exam.

"I'll clear it and get a good rank. How was your dance?" She had previously mentioned that she would be performing a dance at her school's annual festival.

"I won't get anything; it's already over. But that reminds me of you mentioning that you were waiting in front of my school gate on the night of the annual festival. Were you really there?"

"Yes, madam, for three long hours," I replied.

"Where were you? I checked there almost ten times and couldn't see you."

"I was at the gate; where else would I be?"

"Which side?" she questioned.

It was then that I learned about the other gate of her school. How foolish I had been to check only one side of the school! But it wasn't just me; she could have checked the other gate as well, couldn't she?

We engaged in a playful argument to determine which one of us was the greater fool. In the end, we declared it a draw, deeming both of us equally foolish. She didn't seem to mind my eccentricities and appeared to be enjoying my company.

As we neared our destination, I continued to contemplate

changing the venue. However, I had no money and couldn't bring myself to admit it to her.

We were almost there, and I desperately suggested a change in the venue to avoid the embarrassing issue of not having enough money.

"Would you mind if I went to the ATM to withdraw some cash?" I suggested, reaching for my wallet.

"There's one nearby," my tentative girlfriend replied, not realising I didn't even have a card.

"Oh, crap! I guess I forgot my card at home," I said, trying to act nonchalant. She looked at me, probably having already guessed the truth.

"You know, you're quite cute! I invited you, so I'll cover the bill. Why are you worrying so much? Besides, you should know... my dad is loaded!" she reassured me, injecting some humour into the situation.

I experienced a mix of emotions—flattered by her compliment yet also embarrassed by my financial predicament. I wasn't sure if guys were typically described as "cute." I chuckled at her attempt at humour, and soon, we found ourselves inside Café Coffee Day, selecting a table in a secluded corner for privacy.

As we settled in, my nervousness started to grow. We were seated, the menu was placed before us, and I had no idea how to proceed. She looked at me expectantly as if she could read my thoughts. I tried to continue the conversation, but my anxiety caused me to stammer. She pushed the menu toward me and asked me to decide.

I glanced at the menu, filled with unfamiliar items like exotic puffs, pizzas with toppings I'd never heard of, and a bewildering array of coffee options. I felt completely out of my depth and didn't know where to begin. This simple outing had already laid bare my true self, leaving me feeling exposed and vulnerable. I could feel a creeping sense of discomfort washing over me. She, the most beautiful thing that had ever happened to me, sat across the table while I struggled to keep my composure.

Unable to contain my unease any longer, I blurted out a question that was both out of context and intensely personal.

"Do you think we can ever be the way we want to be?"

She gazed directly into my eyes, her expression calm and unfazed by my sudden intensity. Her silence encouraged me to continue.

"I'm not the guy you should go for, Ami. You deserve someone better than me—smarter, more handsome, someone who knows how to take care of you. I come from a remote village; I don't even know the etiquette of being in a big city, especially with a girl. I'm scanning this menu, and I've never had any of these things before. I didn't even have enough money to pay for all this, which is why I panicked before coming here. Someday, you'll find someone better than me. Someday, you'll leave me and go because I know I don't deserve all of this..." I trailed off, my words filled with self-doubt.

Avoiding her gaze, I expected a negative reaction and berated myself for being jumpy with words. But then, she reached out and gently held my trembling hands, which had been tightly clenched in nervousness.

"Nav, I may not have known you for more than 10 months, and we've hardly spoken five times during that period. But trust me, you are wrong about yourself," she said, her voice reassuring. "Not all of us start on an equal footing. Last time we met at the café, if there had been any other guy, he would have probably resorted to cheesy lines or tried to make a move. You did none of that. You simply smiled at me for over 10 months now, and I saw a genuine person every time I looked into your eyes. Contrary to what we often believe, love doesn't happen by chance or at first sight across a crowded school fest. It grows slowly, sinking its roots before branching and blossoming. You'll find that when you love someone, the face becomes less important than the brain, and the body becomes less important than the heart. You have a beautiful heart."

Suddenly, it felt like she was a different person altogether, and I finally met her eyes, which twinkled with sincerity and warmth. She was young but possessed a wisdom far beyond her years, exceeding even my wildest imagination.

And she broke the silence, "Never seen a girl before? Why are you staring at me?" I continued to stare, captivated by her presence. She blushed and lowered her gaze.

"What's your full name, Mr. Tubelight?" she asked playfully.

"Planning to propose already?" I teased.

"I don't know, but you did give a clear 'NO' on our first meeting." Her response was indirect yet revealing. We were beginning to communicate through our eyes. She smiled, looked at me, and then shyly glanced away. I was in a whole new world. Love had found me.

I handed her the slam book, and she started going through my entry right in front of me.

We enjoyed hot chocolate and engaged in a warm conversation. She even taught me how to eat a burger without letting the fillings spill out from the other end. She shared her wisdom on how to stop pretending and how not to get nervous around girls. We talked about nearly everything under the sun. At that moment, I felt complete.

After an hour, we moved to a nearby cyber café with a sign that boldly claimed, "The coolest place to be this summer." We continued our indirect communication. We had waited for 11 long months, and now, face to face, we struggled to find the courage to utter those three little words. I tried to express my feelings by showing her a few e-greetings that said "I love you" during our random browsing session. She had already understood everything but just sat there quietly, occasionally smiling. I gazed into her large eyes, feeling my heart race. In the magic of that moment, I took her hand and kissed it, making her blush.

"I'm going home for 3 days, Ami," I said.

"Today?" she asked.

"No, tomorrow."

"You're coming back, right?"

"I promise," I assured her.

She smiled and said, "Oh, that means I'll have to see you again. How sad!" We shared smiles; our hearts echoed opposite sentiments.

On our way back in the rickshaw, she tightly held my hand. Both of us remained silent, finding solace in each other's touch. She knew I was leaving, and I knew I would have to say goodbye. It was a strange pain, having something you knew you were about to lose. She had given me a new lease on life, a newfound strength. As we approached our colony, her grip on my hand grew tighter. She leaned on my shoulder and whispered, "I'll miss you." I had already started missing her.

That evening, she stood by the main gate of her fence, lost in thought, perhaps imagining how different the place would be after I had left. I watched her from my window, fully aware that I would miss her deeply. She blew me a flying kiss and disappeared inside.

Chapter 14
Results Came in Early

The results of my Manipal entrance examinations, anticipated in about a week, arrived unexpectedly while I was home.

"It's a call for you," my mom said, her face radiating a cheerful smile that left no doubt about the caller's identity. I rushed to the phone.

"Hi, Nav."

"Hi, Ami. How are you?"

"Actually, quite good, now that you're not here anymore. How are you?"

"I cleared Manipal, Ami. I got rank 688."

"Is that good?"

"It's good."

"I always knew you would do well. Congrats, tube light. By the way, how much donation did you give for this rank?"

"Ah! You arts students will never understand this."

"Oh yes, and you will understand everything."

And then there was a pause.

"Okay, tell me, where on earth do you find the most Punjabis?" I tried to change the topic with a joke I had recently learned.

After a moment's pause, she gave the most expected answer, "Punjab?"

"No, madam, in JOKES!"

"Ha ha ha, very funny. Is it okay now?" I was sure she was making faces on her side, but eventually, she tried to spoil the joke.

"You spoil all the fun."

"That's because it's not funny at all. Anyway, leave all this. When are you coming back?"

"Ami, I will come back, but just to pack up."

She fell silent.

"Ami?"

"Yes. I am here," she said, trying to control her emotions, "I see how you are so smart. I just asked you the 'when' thing, and you also replied to the 'why' thing!"

"I am coming tomorrow, Ami."

"For how many days?" No matter how much she tried to hide her feelings, her pretence lacked perfection, and sadness crept into her voice.

"2-3 days."

She fell silent again. I knew what she was feeling.

"Ami, why do you go silent every now and then? Getting emotional? This was bound to happen; I had told you already."

"Emotional, my foot! I am just biting my nails, and Mr. Tube Light, who will get emotional for you? I am happy it's just 2-3 days. After that, I will be free."

"Ami, I want to say something to you."

"Oh really?"

"Yes, I am serious. Are you ready to hear it?"

"Hear what, mister? What's coming up? Let me guess... You love me?"

"Yes, I love you."

There was a long pause.

"Then why did you take so long to say it, Nav?" Her voice changed completely.

"Only if you would have thrown the ball earlier to my house..."

She had no replies. "I will wait for you," she said and hung up the phone.

Chapter 15
Those Three Days

Three days. Just three days, and then the uncertainty of when and where we'd cross paths again. She signaled to me in the morning that she was heading to the Gurdwara and left with her mom. I followed them, accompanied by PK, my unpaid bodyguard.

The Gurdwara, nestled at the end of one of the streets in our colony, wasn't far from our houses and was mostly frequented by local residents. Despite the risk of being caught by someone from the colony, I was willing to take my chances. She instilled a strange confidence in me, and these were the last three days I would gaze into those eyes.

I had never been to a Gurdwara before. Even though it is a spiritual hub for a particular community, Sikhs, it is a very serene and welcoming place with a sense of communal harmony and tranquillity. This one was a big building crowned with a white dome and an ornate entrance leading into a big prayer hall. At one end of the hall was the sacred Guru Granth Sahib, enshrined with reverence. Everyone entering the Gurdwara covered their head as a mark of respect and sat cross-legged on the floor, symbolising equality among all. I covered my head with a bandana that was available at the entrance and walked in.

She occupied a seat at the end on the women's side, and I fixed myself as the last one on the men's side. To my left was only the passage, yet I had to steal glances at her through the corner of my eyes. It felt different, my first immersion into the depth of her community. Many gurus sat at the end of the passage in front of the shrine. Her purple dupatta served as her veil, and every now and then, she would cast a glance at me through its edge. Fear and confidence danced in her eyes. I noticed her palms deliberately displaying 'N' and 'A,' written with mehndi.

She shrugged her head, indicating, let's get out, and while the preaching continued, she got up to leave. Perhaps it might not have been noticed if I had waited a bit before following suit. Unfortunately, we got up almost at the same time, and I caught her mom turning toward me. She must have sensed the disturbance simultaneously at the end of her row and on the men's side. Her round glasses concealed her angry eyes as they were fixed on me. In the next moment, I realised what I should have observed upon entering the place: it wasn't just her mom, but almost all the ladies from the colony were in the Gurdwara. And why wouldn't it be? It was a close-knit Punjabi colony, after all. They were all staring at me. They appeared startled by my presence there. Although a Gurdwara is a place open to everyone at any time, that was the explanation Ami provided later when her mother questioned her about my unusual presence that day. But the people from the colony surely harboured numerous unspoken questions, like 'Why would he come now when he never visited the Gurdwara before?' or perhaps 'Why did they both stand up at the same time?' Without dwelling too much on the situation and its consequences, I did what seemed best at the time—I fled instantly, and Ami resumed her seat.

Those three days were a whirlwind of emotions; I followed her wherever I could, whether it was to the Gurdwara, the market, or the school area—everywhere, just to catch a glimpse of her. We communicated through signals and impromptu phone calls to arrange our secret rendezvous. I didn't care much about what people might think or the potential consequences of being seen together. We met at Café Coffee Day, Jubilee Park, shopping complexes, the temple, and even in the street next to ours at the cyber café.

I gave her a ring as a token of my affection and mustered the courage to ask her to be mine, although, in my heart, I already knew she was mine. She said it would remind her of me when I was gone. Every little effort we made and every moment we spent together brought a unique kind of happiness, knowing we'd soon be separated. Her eyes told me how much she'd miss me when I was gone.

The Last 24 Hours

The countdown had begun. I had a mere 24 hours left in Jamshedpur, and the thought of leaving behind everything I had come to cherish weighed heavily on my heart. In those final two days, we crossed paths countless times. When you know you're about to lose something precious, you want to hold onto it every second, and I was no exception. I yearned to meet her in the middle of the last night I had in Tata. I wanted to stroll down the empty streets that had served as a divide between us for eleven long months when our communication was confined to silent glances. I wanted to walk under the moonlit sky, feeling the cool breeze rustling through her curls and gazing into the loveliest face I had ever known. It was as if I was living in a dream, or perhaps a dream was living inside me. I knew that once I left, every little detail of this place would haunt me, a constant reminder of the most beautiful days of my life spent on that street. She had promised to meet me right at midnight.

I had prepared a few gifts for her: romantic greeting cards, a pair of earrings, a fluffy soft toy 'Bambi,' and an abundance of roses and jasmines. She wanted to visit my room to see the world outside from my window. I had arranged candles on my table, shelves, and in the corners of the room, their soft glow mingling with the fragrance of the flowers. I wanted this to be a perfect date, and she shared the same desire. The day before, when she asked me what I would like as a going-away gift, I replied, "Something that will remind me of you every moment."

I waited in my room, my eyes fixed on the clock. Time seemed to crawl like molasses, and there was still no sign of her. An hour before midnight, I noticed the lights in her room dimming. I thought she would emerge any moment now, but as the minutes ticked away, she didn't appear. Lighting one cigarette after another while waiting, my gaze remained fixed on her gate. I took a stroll around her house, entertaining the notion that she might have fallen asleep, although the probability was slim, considering how significant this time was for both of us. In a desperate attempt to wake her up, I threw some pebbles at her window, just in case she had dozed off. After all, it was our last night together, but alas, nothing seemed to work, and time continued to slip through my fingers.

The digital clock on my nightstand blinked, signaling the arrival of 5:00 am. With a gentle beep, it reminded me of the impending morning. I hadn't allowed even PK, my constant companion and unspoken bodyguard, to sleep. We shared a common sense of melancholy, knowing that the hands of time were slowly counting down to our separation. By evening, I would bid farewell to Tata, a place with many memories.

Morning arrived like a silent whisper; still, there was no sign of her. A sense of sadness washed over me, even though I held onto the belief that she had her reasons. That evening, I was departing, and that being a Sunday, her school was also closed, so the chances of our meeting seemed remote.

At 6:00 am, my phone rang, displaying a local number. It was her voice that greeted me.

"Hello, Nav," she said softly.

"Ami! I waited for you the entire night," I replied, my voice tinged with disappointment.

"I know, tube light, but you can't understand the situation I was in. Everyone at home stayed awake until morning, engrossed in the India vs. West Indies cricket match!"

"Curse those cricket matches! Where are you now?"

"I'm at the phone booth on the first corner, road number eleven. No one at home knows I'm out; they're all fast asleep. Please come quickly."

"I'm on my way," I replied, my heart racing with anticipation.

By 6:10 am, I had reached the designated spot. She handed me a wrapped gift, instructing me to open it later and just talk to her for now. With declarations of love and longing, we exchanged our feelings.

"I have never felt like this before', I told her.

'Neither have I, and that's why let's do whatever it takes to keep it alive.' Her words brimmed with confidence and promise, solidifying my belief that we would find a way to be together again. The future remained uncertain, but at that moment, her unwavering faith gave me hope.

"I will wait for you, Ami," I reassured her, and she, on the verge of tears, managed a joke, "You better do, mister; if you run away, I will come and catch you. Remember, I am the athlete." It was evident she hadn't slept the entire night; her eyes bore traces of her tears. She looked angelic, her hair flowing freely. Her eyes sparkled with each tear she fought back, and she wiped them away with her dupatta.

We both sensed that our time was running out. As the clock struck 6:30 a.m., we found ourselves at the same café where our journey had begun. Despite the early hours, the cleaners were preparing the place for the day. We requested entry, offering to pay double the price, and the cleaners granted our request. Retreating to a private cabin, I held Ami close as she wept, the uncertainty of our future casting a heavy shadow on both of us.

"Will you forget me if we can't meet for a few years?" she asked in a hushed tone.

"Who says that? I will meet you every year until we can be together," I replied, attempting to infuse hope. Deep down, I grappled with uncertainty about how I would manage without seeing her. Four years of engineering college loomed ahead, and she still had to stay in the same place for at least another year to complete her higher secondary education. Maintaining contact through phone calls would be equally challenging, as I wasn't allowed to call her home, and she didn't possess a mobile phone then. The future appeared daunting, and that's why I had initially tried to distance myself, not wanting to give her false promises or hopes. In my belief, love meant trust—a faith you could carry with you for a lifetime.

"Promise me, Nav, you will wait for me," she implored.

"I will," I promised.

We fell silent. A smile played on her lips, an unspoken invitation. Leaning in, the distance between us closed. I could feel her breath on my neck. I reached out, gently tucking a curl behind her ear. In her eyes, I could see a reflection of my nervous anticipation. Time started slowing down, and the ambient noise of the cafe started fading into a hushed whisper. And then, in a moment as delicate as the flutter of butterfly wings, her lips met mine.

It was my first kiss, and I had never imagined it would feel like this. It was soft and tentative to start with but grew deeper and more confident. It was as if all the words we never exchanged were pouring into this single electrifying moment. Every late-night conversation we never had, every secret we never shared, it was all packed in the weight of her lips on mine.

"Oh Fuck". At 7:00 a.m., she nestled against my shoulder, and as I gazed into her eyes, a sudden shock swept over me. I found myself locking eyes with none other than her mother! Yes, her mother!

She peered at us through the tinted glass door of the closed cabin we were in. I knew we were caught; there was no escape. Ami's face drained of color, and she looked as if she might faint at any moment. Her mother stood there, a statue carved from stone, for what felt like an eternity. Both of us were paralyzed with fear. My heart raced at an alarming pace, and Ami's legs trembled beneath her. I held onto her legs tightly to prevent any inadvertent noise. Breathing became an afterthought as we remained frozen. The only sound was the pounding of our hearts as neither of us dared to breathe.

"She's leaving?!" Then, to our astonishment, her mother walked away. She left! We were left in stunned confusion. Various thoughts and fears flooded my mind, making it impossible to ignore them as I continued to stare outside.

This café was not unfamiliar to Ami's parents; in fact, the café's owner was one of Ami's school friend's dad. Ami often visited the café for internet access and photocopies. So, when her family woke up that morning and couldn't find her at home, they began searching for her in the most likely places, ultimately leading them to the café.

"She's gone," Ami's friend announced, knocking on our door from outside.

"But why didn't she say or do anything? She saw us together!" I gasped, still struggling to catch my breath, while Ami remained in a state of shock.

"No, she didn't," her friend explained. She disclosed that the glass was one-way; we could see outside, but her mother couldn't see us.

We both breathed a colossal sigh of relief, the most significant one of my life. Tears welled up in Ami's eyes as she laughed and cried simultaneously. Drenched in cold sweat, I pulled her into a warm hug. This was our closest call yet.

Holding her tightly, I whispered, "If we can escape this, it's a sign that we will be together forever. I promise."

"I will come to see you for the last time today in the evening, and after that, I will never look back. I don't even want to imagine the place without you," Ami said. She entrusted all the letters and gifts I had given her to her friend at the café, intending to retrieve them later. Empty-handed, she left my side. I had no idea what excuse she was going to offer at home to account for her whereabouts.

"Take care, duffer. You'll meet so many girls in college; don't forget me," she said.

"I love you, Ami, and I'll be with you until the end of time." She hurried back to her home, presumably crafting an explanation. At one point, she paused, turned to me, smiled, and appeared to want to say something more but ultimately decided against it. I stood there, watching her disappear from sight.

My time at Tata had come to an end. It was evening, and I sat inside the taxi, ready to depart for the train station. She stood by the gate of her home, dressed in a sea-green suit with a sky-blue dupatta, her hair flowing in the breeze. It felt like I had first seen her outside my window just yesterday. However, her smile was now absent, and she didn't attempt to conceal her tears. Her family, including her mom, witnessed the emotional scene, but no one said a word, as they all understood that my departure was imminent and it was goodbye forever.

PK, my loyal friend, stood beside the taxi. The atmosphere was heavy with emotion, and tears flowed freely from everyone, even my landlady, for reasons I couldn't quite comprehend. As the taxi began to move, I silently watched the familiar street recede, along with the houses, the children, the trees, and most importantly, her. Ami remained standing there until everything disappeared from my view. I felt a lump in my throat, a poignant mix of beautiful memories slipping into an unknown future.

I left Tata behind. And Ami? I didn't know.

PART II
(RUST)

Chapter 16
Summer 2006: The Time Apart

After leaving Tata, life took a downturn for us both. I sought solace in reading the extensive letter Ami handed me on the day we parted. It was a chart paper-sized letter that I revisited countless times. I cherished her promises and spent hours gazing at the two precious hard copies of photos I had of her. Digital cameras were not yet common.

Communication became a challenge. Calling her house was not an option, and she faced difficulties contacting me as well. Mobile phones were just becoming mainstream, and we relied on phone booths for long-distance calls. Summer vacations had started in her final year of high school, and she couldn't find regular excuses to call me from a phone booth or get enough pocket money for daily calls.

I spent my time at home, with the next item on my agenda being the start of college. There was no more Street No 12, no more glimpses of her through my window, no sweet smiles, no hiding from her mom, and no more watching her go to school. Those days, I missed her the most, and the absence of her laughter left a void in my life.

Meanwhile, PK remained in Tata, awaiting the results of his examinations. He kept me updated about Ami, but I knew he would be leaving soon as well.

To alleviate our situation, I sent Ami money through PK, enough for her to buy a cellphone. It wasn't an easy feat, but PK managed to make it happen. Ami, new to the Internet world, convinced her mom during her summer vacation to let her visit an Internet cafe regularly to learn about emailing and more. She convinced her mom that it was a practical skill and a productive use of her time. She would mail me daily, and I would read those emails on a mobile phone that opened Yahoo emails like a text message.

I vividly recall the first email she sent me.

Hello Nav,

I miss you deeply and love you more than words can express. Remember the message I sent you from my dad's cell that you couldn't receive completely? I wrote about the four essential qualities that should exist between two people for a relationship to thrive: true love, faith (or trust), friendship, and understanding. You possess all these qualities, and I consider myself incredibly fortunate to have you in my life. I'm willing to do anything for you; that's my promise.

I understand adjusting to your family might be challenging because our religions differ. Still, I want to reassure you that I will never intentionally hurt you or your parents. Please trust me on this.

Yesterday, despite the heavy rain, I had a wonderful time with my cousins at the amusement park. We even went boating in the rain, and I ended up completely soaked. Now, I have a fever, cough, and a cold, but I'll be fine. On the 16th of this month, we plan to visit the same place again.

I really miss you here, and I've stopped walking in the evening in front of your room. It's painful to be there without you. I love you deeply and miss you more than words can express. I know it is futile, but I wish to say, "Come back."

I'll be leaving soon, but I'll call you on Tuesday, the 11th, at 1:45 pm. Please answer the phone. I get nervous when your mom answers. I love you, love you, love you, and I will always love you until the end of my life. I promise. Bye.

I'm sending you a poem that I wrote for you. I don't know how good it is, but it comes straight from my heart with all my love.

"I THINK OF U"

I think of u if I have a secret to share,
I think of u if I have a moment to spare,
I think of u when I can't sleep,
I think of u when I have a reason to weep.
I think of u if I need a friend,
I think of u when my happiness seems to end
When I feel like holding someone's hand,
And I really need a person to understand
Not only my words but my silence, too,
There's nothing that I can do but think of u.
Whenever there's something I can't decide upon,
I think of u, and the problem is gone.
I rest assured that I'll never be alone when u r near,
Thanks for your presence even when u r not here!
Tell me how you liked it, Your Barbie.

Every day of that summer, I eagerly awaited noon because I knew her email would soon land in my inbox. Her messages never failed to bring a smile to my face. Despite the miles separating us, our love grew stronger daily. Then, one day, she obtained a SIM card registered by the rickshaw driver who took her to school. This simple act of generosity by her rickshaw driver significantly reduced the pain of the physical distance between us. We now communicated through emails and text messages. She would hide her cell phone in her school bag and switch it off during the day. At night, when everyone in her house was asleep, we would have heartfelt text conversations. Calls were still expensive and saved for special days.

A month later, I left for Manipal to join Manipal Institute Of Technology.

Chapter 17
Manipal 1st Semester

Rains of 2006

Getting admission into MIT was a significant milestone for me. Unlike the rest of the gang chasing the IIT dream, my sights were set on Manipal right from the start. Perhaps it was because my brother spent his college years there, or maybe deep down, it didn't matter to me where I went; having fun was a bigger motivation. His stories about the place had turned it into my dream, too.

So, on a rainy August morning, I embarked on my journey to Manipal, laden with bags and hopes of starting a new four-year chapter as an undergrad. The one-day train ride from my village concluded with a stop at LTTE station in Mumbai. From there, with a change of trains, it sliced through the Western Ghats, creating an epic journey for another day and a half. It was then that I understood why my brother couldn't stop talking about the place—it was simply breathtaking. The train traversed dense forests, lush vegetation, mountains and mountains, random waterfalls peeking through them, hills covered with coffee and tea plantations now and then, and tunnels. That journey had 47 tunnels or so before we reached.

India is a big and beautiful place. This marked my first encounter with the south of India, and it exceeded my expectations. Calm backwaters, rain-fed streams, and greenery everywhere—it was serene, peaceful, and practically picture-perfect. Gazing out from the train, I saw rolling hills, misty mountains, and forests so green they seemed to be breathing. The sun peeking through rain-fresh leaves, the vibrant play of colors—it was alive. Everything was.

The houses, adorned with mossy charm, twinkled with life, appearing cozy and cute. The paths, cleansed by the rain, and the roads, weaving through the landscape like ribbons, invited you to wander and get lost.

Manipal pulsed with life, from the stone walls to the thick moss glowing in the twilight. It felt like stepping into a living, breathing postcard.

Nestled in a cocoon of nature, that place with beaches experienced the best of monsoon rains. Its mesmerizing greenery had the power to make you fall in love at first sight. India boasts many beautiful regions, but I had never seen a place as alive and breathing.

The University campus felt like entering a whole new world—it was vast! The place was a university town sprawling across acres located on a hilly cliff. And beaches? There were several nearby. The weather was cool, with low-hanging clouds almost every day, and when it rained, it poured. The wind had a moist and fierce wildness to it—apparently, one of the best monsoons they'd had in years was that rain of 2006.

Within the campus, there was this valley known as the "endpoint". It was the perfect spot to catch the sunrise or sunset over a sea of treetops. Sitting there, everything felt magical, like being in a divine backyard where time stood still. Looking down from that hill, you'd see a river looping around like a blue ribbon on the green velvet of vegetation.

The place teemed with life: people hanging out, some jogging, others strumming guitars, and even a few kicking around a soccer ball. It was like a scene from a movie—so perfect, it always made me miss Ami even more.

Whenever I sat at the endpoint, feeling the sea breeze or watching the rain turn leaves into little streams right outside my window, I wished Ami could see it, too. I wanted to show her every cool spot, from the windy railway bridge over the backwater river to the graffitied desk at the back of my classroom. I guess that's what love is all about—when you find something awesome, you just have to share it with your special someone.

When she entered my life, everything changed. I found this new kind of confidence bubbling up in me—hard to put into words, really. During my first semester of engineering, she'd ring me up first thing in the morning, her voice a wake-up call promising a great day ahead. She'd ask about my day's plan, even though I bet the names of my classes meant nothing to her.

She encouraged me to make friends, both guys and girls. I didn't get why, but she was clever and probably had her reasons. And she had this sweet habit of sending me a song every day.

On weekdays, when she was in school and could sneak her phone out, she'd text me non-stop. She'd share bits of her day, rant about her psychology teacher, or tell me about skipping class for a quick treat—ice cream or pani puri. She'd be bummed if she didn't snag a front seat at her tuition, and she'd get nostalgic passing by my room.

At night, when her house went quiet, we'd chat about everything under the stars. She made this cute rule where I had to sing the song she sent me in the morning. Then, she'd start a word game; she'd say a word, and I'd blurt out the first thing that popped into my head.

She was adorable, my angel.

One morning, she called me up, her voice shaky from tears. She was on her way to school, calling from a payphone, upset and scared because her mom had found out about the cell phone she'd kept hidden for so long. Even though she was frightened, her voice carried this strength, this boldness that made me believe that this girl could handle anything. She was the one reassuring me, telling me not to worry and that things would be okay.

Once her phone was discovered, getting another was out of the question—her parents were keeping a closer watch. So, we got creative with our communication, borrowing friends' phones whenever possible. She'd call me from her friend's phone during evening tuition classes, and every Thursday, as she walked home from school, she'd find a payphone to ring me up—a ritual.

On the mornings of my tests, she'd somehow find a way to wish me luck. She'd occasionally send me messages from her dad's phone, but I knew better than to reply.

My friends from college were lifesavers in one way. They'd help out by calling Ami, pretending to be one of her girlfriends from school, and if the coast were clear, they'd sneak the phone to me so we could have our little chats. Neha was a fictional friend we created.

Living like this was tough; we went from chatting for hours every night to waiting days just to hear each other's voices. Our calls had to be meticulously scheduled, turning into carefully planned appointments. I can still picture her email, the words etched in my mind: "We will talk on 13th November, at 2 p.m. sharp." I clung to those dates and times, eagerly waiting for her call. If she missed one, it was agonising, and my mind would race, wondering what could've kept her from our call.

The first semester flew by, and I was determined to see Ami while heading home. She had a school event on the night I was stopping in Tata, providing the perfect cover for a late-night meet-up. Meeting openly was still off-limits due to her strict family, so we decided on a hotel to avoid any risks. We had planned it all out: she'd look the part of a Manipal student, right down to the backpack, to prevent the hotel staff from getting suspicious.

Seeing her after so long was like stepping back in time. She was tiny, dressed in a yellow Minnie Mouse t-shirt, blue capris, a black cap, and her trademark red school bag loaded with treats. She looked so young, hardly like a 12th grader.

"Nervous?" I asked as I handed her a Manipal bag, part of our ruse. She was to blend in as a student, and I even whipped up a fake college ID for her. We walked into the hotel; the idea was to look like two Manipal students travelling together, with a journey break in Tata. We had about six hours together.

Our hotel rendezvous was nothing like what people might think. We needed a space just for us. She'd brought a photo album full of memories, gifts, and a card that would later decorate my college locker for years.

We spent hours just being close while she took me on a photographic journey through her life, taking me through each and every photo of her in her family photo album. We were talking about everything and nothing. Despite having hardly spent any time together physically, we were still, in a way, just getting to know each other. There was a tenderness in our connection. It wasn't about lust; it was about being together. Time slipped away, and soon, it was time to part. She promised to join me after her exams, her eyes brimming with tears. I believed her because love was the surest bet we had.

As she went her way and I headed to the station to resume my journey home, our bond was clear. We didn't need more than the closeness we shared during that trip. She was my little lady, and I was her engine.

Chapter 18
Times, They Are a Changing

Winter 2007

Returning to Manipal after the semester break, I knew what Ami and I shared was more profound than just physical. We were both eager for her to move from Jamshedpur to a place closer to me. But as time went on, our conversations grew scarce; her preparation leave and the end of tuition sessions meant fewer opportunities to talk. We had to be inventive, sometimes using a friend's phone to connect.

Chatting with her became a rare celebration. My friends could tell I'd spoken to her just by the never-ending smile on my face, visible until sleep claimed me. On the flip side, days without contact left me uneasy, yet the hope of eventually being together was our lifeline. She dreamed of moving to Bangalore, an overnight bus ride away from Manipal, where we could potentially meet on weekends. Moreover, it was the perfect city for her aspirations to become an air hostess.

As days and months slipped by, our sporadic calls—sometimes facilitated by a kind cyber café owner—were like grabbing onto driftwood in the ocean of our longing. They were brief and infrequent, but they kept our hopes afloat.

It was a mystery how she managed to slip out of her house on those class-free days, but she never failed to call me before my monthly exams. She believed in a simple superstition I once shared: hearing her voice before a test always brought me luck.

Her board exam results came out in May. She excelled, surpassing most of her classmates and securing her spot among the top scorers with more than 90 per cent—a significant achievement.

The moment we had both been looking forward to finally approached. It was time for her to step out into the world. She passed an entrance test for a hotel management institute in Kolkata, but attending college there wouldn't change the distance between us. She let that opportunity pass, holding out for the chance to move to Bangalore. However, her family was convinced that Bombay was a better choice, largely because her aunt lived there, and they knew no one in Bangalore. It's natural for parents to want their child in a place they consider safe.

For me, Bombay wasn't too far off either. It was where I usually switched trains during my travels between home and college. If Bangalore was a 12-hour bus ride from Manipal, Bombay was 18 by train, not a big deal, I thought. Little did I know that this small difference in distance was about to bring a significant change in our lives.

She moved to her mom's cousin's place in Bombay in July. Soon after, she started her training at an institute for aspiring air hostesses and also enrolled in a college for her BA. She was thrilled, and so was I. Her excellent 12th-grade marks and sports achievements gave her an edge for college admissions. She didn't hesitate to forgo the business management college spot in Kolkata. Bombay was closer to Manipal, and her goal was to be nearer to me, in a place where we could meet more often.

I was home on my semester break when she moved. About a month later, I had to head back. She still didn't own a cellphone, but we found ways to stay in touch, using her friends' phones during college breaks.

She was flourishing, enjoying her new life and classes. In no time, she picked up the savvy needed for city life—navigating local trains ticketless, shopping smartly, and even bargaining with rickshaw drivers. She was a sharp little one.

Chapter 19

3ʀᴅ Semester | Rains 2007 | 10 Storey Love Song

The train approached Lokmanya Tilak Terminal in Bombay, and I readied myself for a special rendezvous. If not for the plan to stop in Bombay for a day, I would've been on a connecting train to Manipal. I kept visiting the train's bathroom to ensure I looked my best, knowing that this would be the first time we'd meet without the prying eyes of a small town around us.

Both of us held Mumbai in awe, a city of freedom, far from the watchful gaze of her parents and neighbours.

Stepping off the train, I scanned the bustling crowd for her face, half-expecting her to jump out at me with flowers in hand. But as minutes turned into half an hour and she was nowhere to be found, my heart raced with a mix of excitement and concern. She didn't have a cell phone by then, adding to my anxiety.

I stepped out of the railway station for some air and a cloud of smoke, the monsoon sky above threatening a downpour—a familiar scene for anyone acquainted with the Western Ghats during the monsoon. As I fussed with a wrapper stuck to my shoe, my cellphone vibrated with an unknown local number. Instinctively, I knew it was her. Confusion swirled in my mind. 'Why a local number? Couldn't she make it? Was she lost or in

trouble?' Without letting my thoughts spiral further, I answered the call.

"Engine, where are you?"

"Ami, where are you? I've been waiting for ages. Where are you?"

"Don't freak out, Dumbo... It took me forever to find this station; it's on the other side of town from me. I'm here now, hunting for you. Where are you?"

"I'm outside, just... um, getting some air. Which phone booth are you at?"

Tossing my cigarette and sprinting back to the platforms, I knew there were only a couple of phone booths there. She had to be at one of them.

"I'm at the one on platform number one, I think. But I don't see you."

I hung up, and there she was, paying the booth attendant, looking just as she did six months ago in Tata during my first-semester break. The same petite girl I'd spent countless days talking to, evenings mulling over, and nights dreaming of.

She stood there with a big bouquet of red and pink roses wrapped in green and clear plastic, the magic of the moment enveloping us both.

She turned, and in that glance, our eyes bridged the distance between us. It felt like an eternity had passed, yet we stood unchanged. Words weren't needed; our history was rich with silent greetings, each encounter an adventure. Our eyes said it all, reflecting wonder and a shared history, even as the monsoon adorned her with droplets that shimmered like pearls in her hair.

Drawing her close, I kissed her forehead, a gesture familiar yet always new. She handed me the roses, her voice a gentle murmur, "I love you, my engineer, missed you so much."

"We're free now," I said.

"As free as birds," she replied, her hand in mine. At that moment, we feared nothing, fully immersed in a dream that had long thrived in our hearts. The rain outside grew heavier, and we hailed a cab.

"Where to?" I asked.

"You're the local," she teased, her eyes dancing with mischief, clearly enjoying my disorientation.

"Maybe somewhere to eat?" I suggested, trying to find solid ground in the whirlwind of emotions.

She played along, joking about her petite size. "Am I really that small?"

"To me, you're just right," I said, wrapping her in my arms.

From the cab window, she pointed out the landmarks of her new city—the bustling markets, the iconic homes, her institute, and the places she hung out. Each site she mentioned was a chapter in the story she was writing here. She shared her list of spots she'd hoped we'd visit together, and with each word, Bombay felt less like a sprawling metropolis and more like a canvas for our memories.

We buzzed through all her cherished spots in Bombay by day—cosy couple's points, Juhu beach, the cafeteria at her institute, and the luminescent curve of the Queen's Necklace. But dusk approached, and I had yet to figure out where to spend the night. Hotels were out of the question; their steep prices didn't match my budget.

She was living with her aunt in an apartment complex. She spun a wild plan for our night on the rooftop of their 10-story building, and I, ever the accomplice in our escapades, agreed.

"Do you see that aeroplane, Nav?" she pointed skyward. We were up on the rooftop of her apartment with limited access. All we had to do was hit hard on a rusty lock, and the access door opened. She had learned this trick in her short stay there so far.

"Yes, Ami," I responded, following her gaze.

"Someday, that'll be me up there," she dreamt out loud.

"And I'll be here, waving at you," I promised.

"I'll shower you with roses and chocolates from above," she giggled.

"Just don't stick your hand out too far from the window," I joked with a mock stutter, and she beamed.

She was radiant in the soft glow of the evening. We spent long hours talking, dreaming, and commenting on the different buildings we saw from there. Eventually, sometime past midnight, sleep overtook us, and we woke up in a couple of hours with a drizzle. Cold and shivering, we took shelter under the water tank on the roof, each of us holding the other close for warmth. This had been her bold plan—our night under the open sky. Dawn broke soon afterwards, painting the horizon with hues of anticipation. The rain had stopped.

She snuck back to her apartment and soon returned, refreshed. I warmed myself in the newborn sunlight, pacing the rooftop for warmth. We ventured out once more to embrace her city.

She took me to Bandra, the iconic Prithvi theatre. We hung out at Irani cafés and walked along the wall murals. We ran fast, and time ran faster.

That evening, as I boarded my train onward to Manipal, we both sported fevers—souvenirs of our adventure from the night before. Her tear-filled eyes spoke volumes; she had lived her best night. And in her gaze, I knew, so had I.

CHAPTER 20
FLIGHTS OF FANTASY

"I've submitted your air hostess application for an airline."

"What? Now? But I've got like five or six months of training left," she gasped, caught between excitement and panic.

"Why wait if you can ace the interview right now?"

"But I'm not sure I'm ready. I really don't want to fail."

"You're more prepared than you think, and even if it doesn't go perfectly, it's a valuable experience. No need to panic, okay?"

As her interview date approached, I became her makeshift coach over long-distance phone calls. She had managed to own a cellphone by then. I drilled her on everything from dressing right to handling tough questions and even mastering subtle makeup—all credit to a few helpful online searches; the internet was becoming a thing around us. Every night, our singing sessions were followed by mock interviews. It was heartwarming, really, how seriously she took my advice.

November 8th

The big day arrived. That morning, her voice trembled as she described her outfit and makeup, repeatedly questioning whether I believed in her. I did, truly.

10 a.m.

She stepped into her first-ever interview for airlines, and I was a bundle of nerves, silently praying for her success. I hoped she'd clear just a few rounds, enough to boost her confidence. Under my classroom desk, my phone was my lifeline, glancing at it for any update while avoiding the lecturer's eye.

2 p.m.

"Nav! I've cleared the first round!" Her voice was bursting with joy that could outshine any prize I could win.

"I knew you would."

"Thank you, love. I'm off to touch up before grabbing a bite. The next round could be any minute now. I'll call you afterwards."

"Best of luck, Ami."

"Thank you, Nav. You're the one who built this confidence in me."

Inside, I knew that she was the one who had truly changed my life.

8 p.m.

In a heavy and sad voice, she called me, "Nav."

I tried to offer some comfort, saying, "Hey Ami, what's going on? It was just your first interview, and there are more chances ahead. I'm here for you."

And then, like a burst of sunshine, she shouted, "Eeeeeee! I made it through the finals! I'm going to be an air hostess!"

I couldn't believe it.

Ami continued, "I owe this to you, Nav. Everything today happened because of you. I'll call you after I finish the paperwork."

I struggled to find the right words. It felt like I had just won a prize myself. I celebrated with my friends. Ami becoming an air hostess meant stability for her and me, fewer financial worries, and was kind of a validation of our relationship. It was like the start of our dreams coming true. I couldn't help but reminisce about our first meeting in the cyber café in Jamshedpur when she had boldly said, 'I want to become an air hostess; I want to fly.' My girl was a hero.

Her job training was set to kick off in January, and she was knee-deep in medical tests and paperwork hassles. As we started becoming more financially independent, one day, she quietly sent me her internet banking and card details. When I questioned her about it, she chuckled and said, 'Let's share what we make.

And also, the man of the house should keep an eye on the finances.' In reality, she wanted me to feel like it was our money. Who thinks so much? With each passing day, I grew fonder of her charming quirks.

Our relationship had always been an adventure, though we hadn't spent much time together. Now that one of us had achieved our professional dreams, we decided it was high time to simply enjoy each other's company. My winter break was set to start in mid-December, so we planned to spend a day together in Mumbai and then take a train together to go back to our homes, a 2-night 3-day journey together. It presented itself as no less than an all-inclusive getaway resort to us.

CHAPTER 21
WINTER 2007 | TRAINS

Once again, I found myself eagerly counting down the hours until I'd reach Mumbai station. When I arrived in the morning, the weather was surprisingly chilly, with a biting wind that made me feel like a medieval churchkeeper in my black jacket and hood. She bounced toward me as I stepped off the train, clutching a bouquet of bright red and yellow flowers wrapped in transparent paper, just like the first time we met. In a burst of spontaneity, I planted a kiss on her lips in public for the first time, and her response was, "Why do you look like an alien?"

"Shall we?" She asked.

"Of course, madam," I replied with a grin.

She walked beside me with an air of pride that mirrored the feeling I had. We hopped into a cab and asked the driver to find us an affordable hotel. Unfortunately, there was a yearly jewellery exhibition in Mumbai on those dates, and all the good hotels were fully booked. How and why would I have known that in advance? The few available options were exorbitantly priced, nearly wiping out our combined pocket money. We wandered from place to place, trying to find a room. Two of her fingers were crossed over one another till we found a reasonably priced place. We settled for a rather basic lodge, and even that was freakin costly.

As soon as we entered the room, she enveloped me in a tight hug as though she had been waiting to do so for ages. She was on the cusp of becoming a real air hostess. It felt like we were halfway there.

"I'm going to tell my mom about us now," she said.

"Is this the right time?" I hesitated as thoughts of her mom sent shivers down my spine. Her mom's disapproving gaze, hidden behind round glasses perched on her shiny nose, was what came to mind whenever I thought about her.

"Yes, Nav, it's been too long. I'm not afraid of anyone now. You've made me realise my dreams, and they'll understand me."

"But shouldn't you have asked me first?" I quipped, trying to lighten the heavy air.

"Why? Are you planning to run off with someone else?"

"What if I do?"

My comment, which I didn't consider particularly serious, acted as a catalyst. After some intense emotional turmoil, all happening within a fraction of a second, tears streamed down her cheeks. I was taken aback.

"Please, never say that, even as a joke," she almost pleaded and told me how she couldn't bear the thought of living without me. It would have made me laugh if I didn't love her so deeply. Instead, I gazed into her tearful eyes, grateful for her innocence and love.

The rest of the day was spent in the room, exchanging countless kisses and embracing each other. She lay beside me, her fingers tenderly caressing my hair as we talked about our future. She shared her vision of our wedding, considering her Sikh heritage and my Hindu background. In her tradition, marriages happen during the day, and in mine, it is an overnight ceremony. We playfully debated whether to hold the ceremony in the evening or, in her words, 'keep marrying day and night.'

I cherished these silly arguments with her. She spoke about her dream of travelling to the Cape of Good Hope with me and staying at a high vantage point surrounded by water. She was unlike anyone I had ever known and was made up of innocence and dreams. That night, she curled up beside me like a baby. I couldn't sleep; I simply watched her peaceful face, occasionally brushing her eyelashes or touching her ears, which caused her to react even in her sleep. Sex? Both of us wanted. None of us knew. So, we made out and made out, and made out, all night long.

The next day, we boarded a train. She had brought along a deck of cards for a game of UNO, which surprisingly remained the highlight of her day. To my amazement, she won every time, teasing me with playful faces and claiming that engineering alone couldn't rule the world. I suspected the game might have been rigged, or she had another deck hidden. We sat facing each other by the window, the chill in the train compartment making us huddle under the same blanket. Every now and then, she would sneakily pinch me with her feet, then feign innocence when I looked at her.

As the journey progressed, we alternated between silence, gazing at the world outside through the tinted glass, and our lively card game. Topics shifted effortlessly, and at one point, I explained how embedded systems worked, with tiny electronic chips inside everyday objects. She speculated whether she had an electronic chip inside her to control her actions, and her imagination ran wild with thoughts of programming someone's electronic chip in their head. I had to gently tell her it was impossible, to which she responded with a yawn. She had a wild mind. Our journey was far from over, with her in the upper berth and me in the lower one.

Indian long-distance coaches have capsule-like space in a train with snug berths in neatly draped clean linens. It is a mix between a compact hotel room and a shared cabin, offering both privacy and a chance to socialize. Ours was a bunk bed behind a set of curtains.

In the middle of the night, I woke up to find her sleeping beside me. I was both thrilled and puzzled, but thanks again to the curtains, we had privacy. Still, how she had managed to sneak into my bed without a sound was rather amusing. She was fast asleep, her grip on me loose. Whenever the train passed a lamppost outside, the shimmering light would reveal her radiant face, and I couldn't resist gently kissing her closed eyes. I felt like the luckiest person on Earth.

The next morning, she explained with a mischievous smirk that she ended up in my bed because she was too tired to climb back up to her berth after a late-night trip to the restroom.

"What else could I have done? I had no other option!" she said, using exaggerated hand gestures and a serious expression to emphasise her point.

She woke up her playful self in the morning, and through the day, as the time of her arrival in Tata drew near, she grew quieter. She would become subdued when she was sad.

"Thank you, Nav," she said.

"I've told you before, you don't need to thank me for anything. "

"This time that I am home, I'm going to tell my mom about you."

"And I'll always be here for you, Ami. You can tell that to your mom, too."

"Anything else you want me to tell my dear engine?"

"Oh, yes! Tell her that we plan to name our daughter 'Little Ami.'"

"Really? I'd prefer a tiny Nav instead."

I looked deep into her eyes and asked, "But how are we going to make that happen?" Both of us were so naïve at lovemaking.

She blushed so deeply that it seemed her face might burst. That night, I didn't sleep on my bed. Once all the other passengers were asleep, we held each other tight.

And everything happened. Everything. Everything that hadn't happened in closed hotel rooms in Mumbai, Jamshedpur, or the secluded cabins of cyber cafes.

In the softly lit train compartment, with the world outside whizzing past as a dreamy blur, that evening, magic was unfolding for us. I gazed into her eyes, feeling a flutter of excitement and a sprinkle of nerves. It felt like we were stepping into a story we had only imagined before, but now it was real, gentle, and as fresh as a winter night.

Our hands found each other, fingers intertwining in a gentle, tentative embrace. Each touch was like an unspoken word, a silent conversation held in our shared gaze. The soft rhythm of the train seemed to shield us from the world, creating our own little universe where time stood still.

I brushed a strand of hair from her face; her curls were like cotton. Her warm, reassuring smile calmed the sea of emotions inside me. As we leaned closer, the distance between us just melted away. It started with a kiss, filled with the innocence of first love, sweet and unhurried. We made love.

In that snug little compartment, we found a wonderland in each other, a connection beyond words, woven from trust, understanding, and the softest touch of affection. As the train hummed on, we sat together, wrapped in a comfortable silence, our hearts beating in harmony with the rhythm of the rails.

Chapter 22
Flying in a Blue Dream | 4th Semester | 2008

We were both in our hometowns, soaking up the joy of our respective vacations after an adventurous journey. I had a full month of holiday bliss, and she just had two weeks before she returned to Bombay to begin her airline training. One night, during the vacation, the phone rang around midnight, and her voice came through all happy and chirpy.

"I spilt the beans to my parents!" she announced with excitement.

"How did they react?" I asked.

She chuckled, "Well, when I told them I am in love with you, Mom blushed like she was the one head over heels for you, and Dad quickly exited. But after I gave them the whole spiel about how your support turned me into this proud Air Hostess and how it's not just a teenage crush, Dad started to thaw. Don't worry; he'll come around. Mom even claimed she remembers your face!"

I breathed a sigh of relief because I'd always feared her parents might be the tough nuts to crack.

"So, did you mention that I'm Hindu?" I inquired.

She replied, "Oh, come on! My parents aren't living in the dark ages. They're cool with it."

Grinning, I pushed my luck a little further, "And did you spill the beans about our train adventure?"

There was a mischievous pause on her end, and I could almost see her blushing. "Are you trying to get me in trouble? Do you want them to disown me?" she teased with a hushed voice.

It turned out her parents were incredibly proud of her, and as long as she had their trust, they were on board with her choice of being with me. Her parents, like any good parents, just wanted to shield their daughter from life's curveballs. Her entire family embraced me exactly as Ami presented me to them, and I couldn't have been happier. On my end, things were smooth sailing. My parents were open-minded; my brother was already in the loop, and he even chipped in secretly to cover my extra expenses for love-related affairs. Mom had an inkling about her, and there were no hurdles on my side.

As she left for Mumbai after a few more days at home, I stayed behind, soaking up the last bits of my vacation.

The Fellowship of the Rings

On my way back to Manipal, during a short stop at Bombay station, where I had to change trains for the onward journey to Manipal, we had a precious two-hour window together. I had a surprise for her, or so I thought.

"I have something for you," she said.

I took my best guess, "Hmm... let me guess, another teddy bear?"

"No, you dumb ball of yarn, now you are a grown-up guy; you don't need that anymore. You have me instead...now close your eyes first."

And then, like a magician revealing a surprise, she slipped a ring onto my finger. As I opened my eyes, hers locked onto mine. She had another ring in her hand, ready for action. Without missing a beat, I grabbed the ring and slid it onto her finger, right there on the railway station platform. It was like a private engagement ceremony at an extremely public place, with about 20 of my engineering friends, who were also travelling to college, gathered around us with their luggage. My friends were our cheerful witnesses. The railway station, usually a place for rushed goodbyes and hurried reunions, became the stage for a heartwarming and unforgettable chapter in our love story. She pulled me into a warm hug, her eyes filled with playful curiosity, silently asking, "What's our next adventure, partner-in-crime?"

Her airline flight training had already commenced. She had to complete a five-month training program before being assigned to a real route. The training facility was quite far from her current accommodation at her aunt's place, so she moved to a PG closer to the training centre. She became busier with her training, and although I missed our spontaneous conversations, I appreciated that it was all for our shared future.

As things changed, it became clear that any change for the better was welcome. Our increased happiness and the satisfaction of our relationship came at the cost of the time we used to spend chatting on the phone. Her hectic schedule left little for late-night conversations, but whenever we talked, she'd share details about her aviation classes, the commands she was learning, and everything related to her training.

Then, a significant date approached—Feb 13th, a day before Valentine's Day. She was scheduled to visit Manipal for the first time, fulfilling one of our dreams. It was an anticipated moment for both of us. Manipal, with its breathtaking natural beauty, was the most enchanting place I had ever been, and she was the most beautiful girl I knew. I had already booked her train tickets and sent them to her. She had managed to take two days off from her training for this trip.

She waited at the station for her train to arrive. Just moments before her train was due to pull in, we were on the phone, and I was giving her last-minute advice for her first solo journey. She was all set. However, around half an hour later, she called me

with a heavy heart, and it was a shock to my system when she told me that she had missed her train.

"You missed the train? How is that even possible? You were at the station well ahead of time, on the platform! How could you miss it?" I was utterly surprised, confused, and concerned.

Though I knew she had a playful side, I quickly realised this wasn't a prank. She was genuinely upset, and I couldn't help but feel bad for her. Looking back, I can sense that something might have been amiss, but at the time, I had no idea. The only solace was that I had plans to visit Bombay soon.

Chapter 23
Buttons and the Magic |
Spring 2008

A few weeks later, I embarked on a thrilling adventure to the IIT Bombay Tech Fest with two friends armed with our aquatic, wirelessly controlled robot. Our creation was designed to navigate a water maze filled with obstacles both above and below the surface. The IIT Bombay Tech Fest was renowned across the country and beyond for being one of Asia's largest technology festivals. It attracted participants from far and wide, offering a platform for showcasing innovations in science and technology. The campus buzzed with activity, featuring talks by prominent figures in the field and countless students tinkering with peculiar gadgets, accompanied by voltmeters and oscilloscopes, performing mysterious experiments by the roadside. It is as nerd as you can get and as cool as you can imagine. Tough combination, I know.

Securing accommodation on campus required filing an application, a process typically approved for participants from other colleges if submitted in a timely manner. The campus was a melting pot of students from colleges all over India. Our robot had been in the making for quite some time, and there were moments when we questioned whether we'd meet the looming deadline. Thus, the trip to Bombay wasn't set in stone and kept as a surprise for Ami.

However, my plan of surprising her backfired when, on the night I was on the train, and she couldn't reach my mobile, she resorted to calling my roommate. That's how she found out I was headed to IIT Bombay. Instead of me surprising her, she amazed me with her resourcefulness. She had grown remarkably clever. She made her way to IIT Bombay in time, checked the accommodation list at the reception for out-of-town participants, and led herself to the accommodation block where I was staying. Within five minutes of my settling in, she gave me a call, and her timing was impeccable.

I rushed outside to greet her and met with a mischievous smile, a look that seemed to say, 'You can't outsmart me.' I saw her in her professional air hostess attire for the first time. She looked absolutely radiant like she had just stepped out of a glamorous vintage movie. With her hair perfectly coiffed and that charming smile, she could have given any real flight attendant a run for their money. I couldn't resist playing along and asked her for in-flight snacks, and we both burst into laughter. She wore our 'private' engagement ring on her right hand.

My friends who had accompanied me to the competition instantly started calling her "Miss Hostess" when they saw her. It amused me, but it wasn't unexpected.

I proudly presented our robot to her, and we went to the designated area for trial runs. A big, wide-open pool in the evening with loud music playing somewhere in the distance. She even tried her hand at the remote control, delighted as if she'd been given a new toy. The technical jargon about circuits and radio frequencies may have gone over her head, but she relished manoeuvring the robot underwater. We had a blast, chatted with friends, and eventually ventured out of the IIT campus for some snacks.

I noticed her phone ringing incessantly, and she kept declining the calls. When she finally switched off her phone, I couldn't help but inquire, "Why don't you answer whoever is calling you so persistently?"

She replied with a hint of irritation, "Oh, he's just this guy from my airline batch. He has this annoying habit of calling even after you have disconnected the call. He's probably calling to ask where to get the uniform from. You know, we received our uniforms today." Something in her demeanour waved a tiny red flag in my mind, but it was Gone with the Wind soon afterwards.

She later switched her phone back on, and the calls had stopped. She also returned to her cheerful self from that tiny little awkward moment. As we sat enjoying pizza at a nearby Pizza Hut, she dropped a bombshell—I nearly choked on my slice. She expressed her desire to stay with me on the IIT campus.

I exclaimed, "How is that even possible? You are not an engineering student. Where would you stay? Moreover, I was wondering if I could go visit your new living arrangement."

Her response was as casual as her demeanour, "I will stay wherever you are, Engine! I don't need much space, do I? Plus, my new living arrangement is on the other end of the town; it would be a day's affair to go if you want to do it on this trip of yours."

"Ok, that's fair, but how can I register an air hostess for a technical fest?" I quipped, puzzled by the logistics of registering an air hostess for the event.

Her response again, surprisingly simple, was, "I don't know anything about that, and honestly, I don't care even if I have to sleep on the street."

So, that's exactly what we did. For the first half of the night, we roamed the college campus, embracing the excitement of being in a totally new setup. Strolling through a wonderland of dazzling displays and interactive gizmos, each one more mind-blowing than the last. To Ami, people there were like magicians, conjuring up robots, apps, and contraptions that made her wonder, "How on Earth did they do that?"

It was a very vibrant evening. Competitions had students on their toes, competing in everything from coding showdowns to robotics face-offs. We cheered for our friends as they battled it out to become the ultimate tech wizards. There were stalls from different companies, workshops, and seminars to let you in on the coolest tech trends. College rock bands screaming their guts out, and cultural performances added a splash of colour and humour to the mix. That evening was a vibrant, quirky, and downright fun celebration of human brilliance and creativity!

Soon, shows started to wind up, people started to go to bed, and the chilly wind started to pierce through our jackets. We

realised it was time to seek shelter. Among the many empty stalls set up by various companies to showcase their products and services, we picked one that belonged to Google. It was conveniently located by the entrance to the central college building. We found two chairs tucked behind a table and nestled ourselves in the darkness, our impromptu hideaway. As usual, she leaned on my shoulders, and in no time, she was fast asleep.

While sleep eluded me, I found myself watching her asleep. To pass the time, I decided to explore her cell phone. Curiosity led me to scroll through her messages. I had no reason why I did that, but as I delved into her inbox, a sudden shock coursed through me. Earlier in the evening, I had sensed something was amiss, and it turned out I was right. She had been keeping something from me, something that appeared to be of significant concern. Her inbox was inundated with messages from an unknown number, and these weren't messages exchanged between friends. Some of them were disturbingly personal and seemed to be personally directed at her. The messages were vague but carried a tense and insistent tone. It was like one-sided sexting. As I glanced at her sleeping form, my mind was besieged by a torrent of questions. "What is she doing here? What is she involved in?" Doubts began to plague my thoughts.

She woke up, and I still had her phone in my hand. When she noticed what I was doing, her face turned pale. I turned the screen toward her, silently conveying my unease. For a moment, she appeared speechless, but then tears welled up in her eyes.

"I'm sorry, Nav. I was keeping something from you," she confessed.

I had no idea what she was about to reveal, and my continued silence only seemed to intensify her distress.

"Please don't be angry, but there are many things I need to tell you. Promise me you'll trust me," she implored, her voice trembling.

My silence persisted, and it brought her to tears. Deep down, I was hurt, struggling to summon the courage to speak. She continued, her voice fraught with fear, "Since I arrived here, many boys have been making advances toward me. From my college to the air hostess training institute and even at my workplace, there are places where I can't walk down without enduring lewd comments. Life here is challenging. Nav is a big city. People are not kind. Those messages you saw in my inbox—there is this guy at Airlines; he somehow got hold of my number and kept sending those disturbing messages. But trust me, I have nothing to do with it. Please, Nav, trust me."

Then, she mentioned the name of the sender of those messages and said that he had even asked her out. She insisted she had never betrayed our relationship. He had been sending messages and attempting to call her, but she had consistently ignored him. She explained that she had never responded to any of those messages or calls because her friends had advised her not to, fearing the irrationality of people. There was an underlying fear in her voice, suggesting there was more to her apprehension than met the eye.

"Today, when I left training early to meet you, he saw me going somewhere and began calling me, perhaps to find out where I was headed. He has even followed me to my PG. I feel so alone here, Nav, so terribly alone. Where should I go? To whom should I report to? I live in constant fear, Nav, afraid to step out on my PG balcony, terrified of taking the local train, anxious about going to the market, and even scared of attending my classes. Tell me, Nav, what should I do? Tell me," she cried, her voice breaking.

And she sobbed uncontrollably. I felt helpless, unable to offer her any meaningful assistance. I was no hero. She was alone in this big city. I lived more than a day's journey away. I held her tightly in my arms.

"Don't fear me of anything, Ami. Don't hide anything from me. You know how much I love you and how worried I get because of you. I would always understand."

"I'm scared here, Nav. I was afraid you wouldn't understand me. I didn't want you to be frightened and burdened with the thought of me being unsafe here. I'm not lying to you, Nav, but my setup here is so hostile; I hate it. Take me with you; keep me by your side, please."

She clung to my chest, seeking comfort. My anger dissolved, replaced by a profound sense of guilt. She kept crying in my arms for the next half-hour, and I cursed the big city and its neon lights that concealed its darker side. I knew she was just a young girl, and coping with all this on her own would be an immense challenge. I embraced her.

"It's getting too cold here; let's find another place to stay, Ami."

We sought refuge in the Civil Engineering department building at IIT Bombay. It was deserted, likely because it was a cold night, students weren't expected, and the security guards were nestled snugly in their blankets, and nobody noticed us, just walking past them to the building.

In an effort to lighten the mood, I tried to make her laugh, kissed her, and apologised for my shocked response earlier.

For the next three days, we stayed on the IIT Bombay campus, hiding in the different department buildings. The computer science lab was our favourite; you could lock the door from the inside. She attended her training classes during the day while I was engrossed in my events. In the evenings, we explored the neighbourhood's hotspots together. All I did in the back of my mind was to wish for things to get better and curse the fate that had placed her in this challenging situation in Bombay.

Chapter 24
Rain 2008 | sixth semester | Walking down the lane

It has been about six months since I last met her. She finished her training and started flying. Life had gotten busy, mine in studies and her in the job. During the last semester break, I couldn't see her because on both days I was crossing Bombay, she was on duty and in midair somewhere. Different, but life was very exciting. She had just received her first salary, and in her own words, she decided to "set up a date with me" in Manipal. She booked her own train ticket. It was the romantic rainy season. Manipal comes alive in all its glory during the rainy season. The monsoons transform this already beautiful campus into a lush green paradise, making it an enchanting place to be. One of our long-cherished dreams of staying together for more than just a few nights was about to become a reality. We were going to be together for a week, and I had arranged a hotel for us to stay.

I vividly recall the afternoon. Her train was about to reach Manipal. An invigorating scent of wet earth, freshly washed leaves, and blooming flowers filled the air. The station was glistening with rainwater. I was on the phone, chatting with her.

"You're almost here, Ami," I informed her.

With her trademark humour, she replied, "Yes, Engine, I can see the rainforest where you live. Seriously, it's just trees and rain, and the train is still slowing down. Do you even have a station here, or should I be jumping off in the middle of a jungle?"

"Hehehe, very funny. You'll be here in a moment." I could see her train from afar.

She continued to tease, "Yes, I can see the platform now. You jungle people must have put in a lot of effort to clear this space, right?"

"Come to the gate of the compartment," I instructed.

Peacefully, she announced, "I've already been standing at the gate of my compartment with my luggage ever since you called me and said I was about to arrive. It's been over 15 mins. What do you want me to do, jump off the moving train?"

The rumble grew louder; the train inched closer, its front lights piercing through the thick veil of rain mist that hung in the air, creating a magical ambiance. The rhythmic clang of the bell at the crossing signalled its arrival, and the platform started to buzz with energy.

I stood on my tiptoe, craning my neck to see through the rows of doors and windows. I knew she'd be in one of those cars, and I could hardly wait to catch a glimpse of her.

Brakes hissed, the train slowed down, and I saw her among the many faces I had quickly scanned in those 30 seconds. I started running along. People on the platform watched my antics, but she was amused. Looking back, I can't quite explain why I was running; it was pure excitement.

"I know you love me, duffer. Why were you in such a hurry?" she said, stepping out of the coach.

Unable to suppress my enthusiasm, I responded, slightly out of breath, "I couldn't help it. Gasp! I love you."

She said, "And you know what? We have to talk about it, but I don't."

I was like, 'What! ' but she followed it up with a dramatic line, declaring, "I feel you inside me with every breath I take. I am no longer your girlfriend; you are a part of me. And whether we are together or not, I want you to remember me as the girl whom you are a part of." After an awkward pause, even she chuckled at that theatrical declaration.

We made our way to the hotel where we would stay for a week, relishing a well-deserved break. That night, I held her so tightly that I didn't know if I allowed her to breathe. Exhausted, she quickly drifted off to sleep while I watched over her, overwhelmed.

I woke up to the gentle patter of raindrops on the windowpane. It was a cosy morning. When it rained in Manipal, it rained for weeks without a break. Ami was up, gazing at me, her radiant smile brightening the room. She leaned in for a kiss, making me feel like the luckiest guy on the planet, raindrops be damned. We snuggled for a while, and then, with a sincere glint in her eyes, she made an unexpected request. I couldn't help but burst into laughter.

"Are you out of your mind?" I asked, part-joking, part confused.

"Maybe I am," she replied, "The question is, are you going to?"

"Are you absolutely sure? You want us to get married? Today?" I still couldn't digest what I was hearing.

"I don't need to rethink it. That is why I'm here. This is not for our parents; this is for us. Nobody needs to know. I just want to get married to you today," she said, her eyes sparkling with love.

"Well, I was asking if you're sure about being crazy," I said, still trying to understand what just happened.

With our hearts pounding, we got ready for the day, paying extra attention to our appearance as if dressing for a grand occasion. She was in a beautiful white kurta, and I did the best I could with neat jeans and a matching white t-shirt.

It was just 8:00 in the morning, and we left for our unique adventure. The campus wore a vibrant green coat sparkling with the mist of just-halted rain, and we walked hand in hand, savouring the earthy aroma and the distant songs of rainforest birds. It was a perfect setting for what was about to happen.

Our destination was the Krishna temple, a serene spot tucked away within the university campus. As we approached its moss-covered stone architecture and the peaceful pond nearby, a sense of awe went down us. The gravity of our request hung in the air, adding a touch of awkwardness to the nervousness rising in the moment.

Summoning every ounce of courage, we approached one of the young priests who was attending to the temple's sanctum.

We exchanged nervous glances before sharing our extraordinary request. The priest, taken aback and clearly not expecting such a plea from two students looking like kids, gazed at us with wide eyes. His first thought was that it was a prank.

In the temple's hushed surroundings, the scent of incense and flowers wafted through the air as we awaited his response. Our hearts were pounding with hope and apprehension.

"Are both of you of permissible age?" The priest's question held a hint of scepticism, and I couldn't blame him.

His inquiry was perfectly valid, though, and I was relieved to confirm that we were both of legal age. The irony was that Ami, despite her youthful appearance, had passed the age threshold, a fact the priest found hard to believe. To assure him of our sincerity, we offered the temple donation box some green leaves, symbolizing our commitment.

After a moment's contemplation, the priest agreed to help us. However, he had one more condition. He requested to see our birth certificates, a formality to ensure his nose was clean. Thankfully, we had our ID cards with us; mine was real, and Ami's was fake. With a nod of approval, the priest asked us to follow him to a room tucked away towards the back of the temple, where our love story was about to take an unexpected and private turn. In about 20 mins, with an express service, we got married.

In the spirit of honeymoon, we went around the University. We walked to the End Point Valley. It was the end of a plateau cliff, and you could see the river below twisted like a snake through the thick green treetop. Couples, much like us, sat on their own rocks and gazed at the view, students playing football, guitar strums in the air, and motorcycles and cars doing their own stunts. It was the lover's point of the settlement.

We trekked down the edge to a boat in that river. As we clumsily rowed, we couldn't stop laughing at our less-than-perfect paddling skills. I kept reminding her that she was the athlete. It was a mix of splashes and giggles.

We made our way to the railway overbridge somewhere down that backwater river. It was so quiet you could hear a pin drop. We tried whispering and shouting to see how far our voices would travel, shouting 'I love you' at the top of our lungs and getting an echo somewhere from the hills, which was a very empowering feeling. We reminisced about the time that we lived in front of each other for a year and never talked.

In our trek, a wooden hanging bridge over a rivulet was a riot. She was a bit scared at first, but as soon as we started crossing, her fear turned into excitement. Every creak of the bridge had us in stitches, imagining it was talking back to us.

Evening approached, and we made our way to the nearby beach, which is famous for its lighthouse. The climb-up was a mini workout, but we enjoyed our snack break at the top. We were so prepared, much like a couple on their first trip together. The view from the top of the lighthouse was worth it; the sea, the sky, and the whole world stretched out like a panorama to us. We took turns making up stories about what lay beyond the horizon.

That was the most beautiful sunset of my life. There, on the windy top, we just sat and chilled. She leaned on me, and there was no need for words. It was one of those 'perfect' moments. We were just two kids in love, feeling like the luckiest people on earth.

On our first night as a married couple, we treated ourselves in an air-conditioned room. I set the scene for romance with candles and a yellow rose in her hair. The room was filled with a melody of wind chimes swaying gently in the AC breeze. She playfully avoided making eye contact. We made love. Over and over again. I felt the rhythm of her heartbeat. I felt the warmth of her breath; we had become one.

Over those seven days, we cherished the joys of married life. Rain washed the lush green leaves outside. I diligently attended the critical lectures that I had to, and she sent me off with a loving kiss before I left. She would tidy up my clothes and arrange my books at the hotel. I would return from my evening lectures at four every day, having picked up fresh juice on my way. As the day for her to leave came closer, she grew increasingly reluctant to go back. With some resourcefulness, she managed to secure the necessary funds, acquire a medical certificate for being sick, and reschedule her exit flight, granting us an extra two days.

I was 21. She was 18. And we were married. Life was as beautiful as it could be. Little did I know that the days she extended to stay with me were just borrowed time.

I wish we could have lived happily ever after.

PART III
(DIAMONDS AND RUST)

CHAPTER 25
A NEW CHAPTER | 16 YEARS SINCE

I was 21. She was 18. We got married. It's been 16 years since. Life was as beautiful as it could be.

I wish we lived happily ever after.

Ami had a live-in relationship and an affair in Mumbai since you were on Chapter 22. I bet you are going to go back and see where it was. I was in a delusional, one-sided puppy love for a long, later part of this story. It was my first love. Hers too. But she had other plans.

I came to know about it in the third year of my college. It was a set of unfortunate events that revealed itself to me. It took me some time to realize how long and how far I had been cheated upon. The last memory I could trace was the night we were in Bombay, on the terrace of her aunt, under the wide-open skies.

I don't know why everything that happened after that night transpired. Why did she have to continue with me while she had found someone else? Why did she have to go through the ordeal of letting her family know about me? Why did she have to get engaged to me and come down to marry me? I thought about it a lot in the years that followed; maybe it was mercy, or maybe it was guilt. Maybe it was her way of dealing with the fact that somewhere, she was being unfair to me. Maybe she herself was struggling.

We ended the relationship after the cat was out of the bag. I met her once more since our story was over. She had changed her hair colour to blonde. I swear black looked better on her.

For the last two years of my undergraduate engineering life, I found myself alone, my world shattered, and a secret pain hid deep within. I loved her genuinely and profoundly, believing she was my true love. She had betrayed me. Her infidelity sliced through my trust, through my whole life's construct. The same memories that were happy once were just poisonous now. Without her, my life had so much empty space, uncomfortable empty space.

In the company of my friends, my eyes would often wander to avoid contact. But the words that escaped my lips were not of betrayal but of loss—a different kind of loss. I told my friends that she was no longer of this world, a lie easier to bear than the bitter truth. For in admitting her betrayal, I would have to confront my own vulnerability, my misplaced trust, and the gaping wound in my heart—the shame. The pain was unbearable, the kind that hollowed you out, leaving an echo of what used to be happiness.

The lie was a shield, a barrier against the questions and the sympathy that would inevitably follow the truth. It was easier to speak of her as gone forever than to admit she had chosen another over me. What hurt most was the level of pretence that was put into our relationship toward the end. In my fabricated reality, I found a twisted solace, for in this version of events, she had not rejected me, but fate had torn us apart. I didn't have to face shame. I mourned not just the loss of her but the death of the trust and love I had so innocently given. Each time I spoke the lie, it was a reminder of what I had lost, a reinforcement of the pain, but it was the only way I could cope.

Yet, in the quiet of the night, whenever I was alone with my thoughts, the truth clawed at me. The memories of our time together, once sweet, turned bitter. And that's a fundamental change to one's reality. I grappled with questions without answers and a sense of betrayal that lingered like a persistent shadow. I slowly started turning into a bitter person. I started changing at a very fundamental level.

My friends, unaware of the true depth of my suffering, offered words of comfort for a loss that was not real. And I, trapped in his web of lies, nodded along, a hollow ache within me where my heart used to be. The lie was a fragile bandage over a wound too deep, a wound that time alone could not heal.

For in pretending she was dead, I was trying, in my own way, to bury the part of me that still loved her, to lay to rest the dreams we had shared and to somehow move beyond the betrayal that had changed everything. But in my heart, I knew the truth: she was alive, just not with me, and that was a reality far harder to face than any fiction I could create. When I look back at that time now, I realise that time moves at a different speed when you are in pain like that. I was faced with a very silent grief, and I let it consume me.

Slowly, the lie began to erode me from inside. It eroded my relationships with my closest friends. It eroded my sense of confidence, my self-respect, my ability for joy. It started poisoning my life.

I became a recluse, haunted by the falsehood I had created. Every interaction with my friends was laced with the guilt of my deceit. It felt as if I was living in a parallel world, one where I was mourning a loss that never happened while simultaneously grieving the real one. My avoidance wasn't just about keeping the lie intact; it was a defence mechanism. The more I avoided them, the less I had to face the reality.

Sensing the change and growing distance, my friends started to drift away. They were unaware of the internal turmoil I was experiencing. The isolation I imposed on myself only deepened my distress, creating a cycle of avoidance, loneliness, and depression.

The period of my life that followed was a stark lesson in the consequences of not facing reality. My inability to be honest with myself and my friends cost me valuable people who cared about me. In trying to shield myself from one pain, I had unknowingly inflicted another far more enduring kind of suffering. Today, I realise that just because of this, I have way fewer friends from my undergrad than I should have had.

Two years later, I moved to Bangalore, seeking a fresh start after engineering. The vibrant city, full of opportunities, seemed like the perfect place to bury my past and rebuild. However, the wound inflicted by my own deceit was too deep, and I found myself too weak to confront it head-on.

Over the next half a decade, loneliness and depression clung like shadows, and in a desperate bid to numb the pain, I turned to alcohol and drugs. My job as a software engineer became the only stable aspect of my life, a lifeline that paradoxically enabled my destructive habits. The structured environment of my work and the good income allowed me to maintain this dangerous lifestyle without immediate consequences. As I delved deeper into this dual existence, I began losing touch with reality. On the surface, I was a competent professional, but beneath, I was spiralling out of control, adrift in a sea of intoxication and denial. My colleagues and acquaintances saw only the facade I presented. This secretive double life I led was a lonely journey, a long lonely journey, a path that took me further away from healing and deeper into a world where the lines between reality and illusion became increasingly blurred.

It was a particular evening; there was a palpable shift in the atmosphere. The sky was violet and orange, and a mischievous breeze seemed tousled my hair. It was as if the universe was orchestrating a spectacle, and I happened to be in the audience. I was randomly walking through a nearby market in Bangalore, and my aimless steps turned into an art store. Something seemed to call me from amid the chaos. I stepped inside, and it felt like entering a different world. The walls were covered with canvases painted in vivid colours and shelves lined with tubes of paints and rows of brushes in every size imaginable.

The store was a cosy haven; the air was thick with the scent of paint and old wood, oddly comforting. It smelled like a memory. As I walked through the aisles, my fingers trailing over brushes and canvases, I almost bumped into an elderly man, the store owner. He had such kind eyes that you usually don't see every day. The smile he carried could light up a dim room.

I don't know what happened at that moment, but I just stopped. I stopped to talk to him. I felt like I wanted to. Our conversation started with casual pleasantries; he asked me why I was there. And I told him I didn't know. He asked if I wanted to buy anything. And I told him I was not an artist. And he laughed. We talked for a bit. Mostly about art. But it happens sometimes in life that you get exactly what you need, just not in a way that you'd expect it. That conversation was the therapy I needed at that time. It was a very generic conversation, but I think it is more often than not about the energy you communicate than words. He spoke of art not just as a form of expression but as a connection back to one's soul, a way to light up the darkest corners of our existence. And he spoke with the kind of joy which can invoke joy in someone.

Suddenly, I noticed that he had only one foot. I had been so consumed in conversation that I just didn't notice it up until that point. His other limb was prosthetic. And it just came out of my mouth, 'your feet,' I paused; I didn't know what else to say.

He smiled and said, 'I am standing, am I not?' His words struck something somewhere inside me. We talked a lot. I took a cart, and we went around all the isles. After hearing how he lost one of his feet in a train accident as a kid, we digressed. He told me about Zen, an intriguing concept where the act of painting was more about the process than the outcome, a journey of self-discovery and mindfulness.

We stood by an active canvas in one of the areas of the store, and as he spoke, he moved his hands effortlessly over one, creating strokes that seemed random yet formed something harmonious. There was a thing about his movements, a silent dance between his soul and the canvas. I watched, mesmerised.

"What you see in art is a reflection of what is within you," he said. "Art is not just about creating; it's about finding the light within the chaos, the calm within the storm."

That day, something shifted within me. The encounter, brief as it was, ignited a spark I hadn't known was there, a flicker of playfulness long dormant under the weight of my struggles.

I made a massive purchase. Canvases, paints, brushes, easels—everything I would have needed to get started on this new journey. That night, I returned home and, in a symbolic act of rebirth, I cleared my house of all the bottles of alcohol, drugs, cigarettes, lighters, and all the tangible evidence of my pain and isolation. Was it a day's journey? That's a story for another time, but that evening did set me on one.

With a blank canvas before me, I picked up a brush for the first time. It was awkward at first; the brush felt foreign in my hand, but as I touched it to the canvas, it was cathartic. To just put a blob of paint on that neat white canvas felt like an act of defiance to the void. Each stroke was a release, a way to channel something I had bottled up for so long. The more I painted, the more I found myself getting lost in the colours, the forms, and the act of creation. It was therapeutic. A naïve excitement started coming back to life.

Heartbreak and pain, as harsh and unwelcome as they were, unexpectedly became the forge where art in me was born. In my journey through the art world after, I met countless souls, each with a story of pain to tell. I think that is the poet's curse. During my early days, each tear, each moment of despair, contributed to a well of emotions that I didn't know I could tap into. My heartache became my muse, guiding me to express what words could not. I made a lot of paintings.

Art was healing me. I can only tell in hindsight. The act of creating something new allowed me to slowly accept the pain, even if it was in my suppressed memories. Sometimes, I painted gradients, and sometimes, it was chaos. Sometimes, it was a set of eyes and faces that were merging into each other and yet looking at me. It allowed me to confront my pain in a way that was psychedelic and yet not a negative spiral. It became my lifeline, pulling me back from the brink of self-destruction.

Over the next decade, I made paintings. I painted many things.

The more I created, the more I understood myself. My art was not just about the pain; it was about survival, finding beauty in the midst of suffering, and transforming life's existential agony into something meaningful.

As time passed, the canvases began to fill my home. Painting transformed from a mere hobby to a passion, a vital part of who I was becoming. It grounded me and gave me a sense of purpose and identity that I had lost in the haze of alcohol, drugs, and lies. In art, I found a way to reconnect with myself and, eventually, with the world around me. Art is more than just paint on canvas; it is a path to redemption, a way of rekindling the light that often dims in men. A process of zooming back into present. My paintings captured all the madness, all the anguish inside me. That's why when I look at my portfolio today, I don't see an evolution of art; I see an evolution of me. I see a story. I see unfinished business, I see chaos, I see memory patterns, I see trees. I see a colourful story of light and hope that I must share.

Sometimes, as people, we get into a narrow space to hide from the pain. It starts as a safe space to retreat to. But eventually, it becomes a trap, and it traps our true selves.

Nothing is worth caging your true self.

Absolutely nothing.

Fly. Roar. Breathe.

Do whatever you want to do. Just don't let your life wither away in nothingness. Enjoy small things. Especially the small things.

May you have a good Life.

EPILOGUE

Daffodil Studios

'It's beautiful,' she said, finishing with the last chapter. My therapist had read everything but the ending long ago. 'How do you feel?' she asked.

Me: Honestly? Relieved. But it's a bit empty. If that makes sense, it has been a big part of me for so long.

Therapist: It makes perfect sense. But let's focus on achievement. You concluding this story is one. What helped you finally cross the finish line?

Me: I think it was our conversations.

Therapist: How does it feel to confront reality?

Me: Scary but also liberating. I had been holding my breath for such a long time, and now I can exhale. I had let that narrative of pain subconsciously hold me hostage for so long.

Therapist: But we could see it in your paintings, remember? You could see it as well. I think it was not all me. I just helped you cross the finish line, but all along the way, your art helped you.

Me: I know what you mean.

Therapist: Who do you think you are now that you closed a big chapter of your past?

Me: Not sure. But I am not in a rush to find out.

Therapist: How do you feel?

Me: Life is good.

As I look back at the time when I wrote the first 24 chapters of this book, I feel the pain that the early 20s version of me went through. I want to smack that guy on the head and ask him to wake up. I wish I had not wasted so much time in self-denial and addiction. It was a good love story, but what followed was the real low of life. But even though I wish I hadn't wasted so much of my life, I had a phase where the pain seemed insurmountable, a time that felt like the lowest point in life, and everything had come to an end; it is only in hindsight that I can see how my journey through heartbreak and healing shaped me, allowed me to grow.

To bounce back, you have to hit the ground hard.

I wrote this book, the first 24 chapters, in an attempt to preserve my memories during my years of addiction. Today, more than a decade later, I share this story not just as a conclusion of my therapy but as a message of hope. I want this story to serve as a reminder that even in our darkest moments, there is potential for beauty, growth, and transformation that we often take ourselves too seriously. Nobody can shield you from the pain that life brings you, but I wish that every trial you face strengthens you. I wish that you could take yourself a little less seriously.

I am Navneet Nishant, and this is my story.